God in Her Midst

FEB 2007

God in Her Midst

Preaching Healing to Wounded Women

Elaine M. Flake
Kathryn V. Stanley, editor

JUDSON PRESS
PUBLISHERS SINCE 1824
VALLEY FORGE

God in Her Midst: Preaching Healing to Wounded Women

Judson Press has made every effort to trace the ownership of all quotes. In the event of a question arising from the use of a quote, we regret any error made and will be pleased to make the necessary correction in future printings and editions of this book.

Unless otherwise indicated, Scripture quotations are from the New Revised Standard Version Bible, copyright 1989, Division of Christian Education of the National Council of the Churches of Christ in the United States of America. Used by permission. All rights reserved.

Scripture quotations marked KJV are from The Holy Bible King James Version.

Library of Congress Cataloging-in-Publication Data
Flake, Elaine McCollins.
God in her midst : preaching healing to wounded women / Elaine M. Flake; Kathryn Stanley, editor. — 1st ed.
p. cm.
ISBN 978-0-8170-1506-0 (pbk. : alk. paper) 1. African American women—Religion. 2. African American women—Religious life. 3. Women in Christianity—United States. 4. Spiritual healing. 5. Liberty—Religious aspects—Christianity. I. Stanley, Kathryn. II. Title.
BR563.N4F523 2005
253.5'208996073—dc22   2006034761

Printed in the U.S.A. on recycled paper.
First Printing, 2007.

Contents

Foreword

My introduction to womanist and feminist theology occurred on the campus of Howard University Divinity School. Dr. Kelly Brown Douglas, then my systematic theology teacher, introduced her spring class to the foundations of these theologies. Because of my own church upbringing and the gender equal environment it displayed to me everyday, I struggled then to see the value of including these theologies in our class discussion of liberation theology. After more than twenty years of preaching, with much of the calendar year including time standing in pulpits across the country, I have grown to understand the need to wed these theologies to grow a more effective African American church…that there could be no real discussion of the eradication of oppression for African Americans without also admitting that one of the oppressors of African American women is the African American church itself.

Dr. Elaine Flake is right when she suggests that our preaching must be aimed at setting *all* oppressed people free—including those oppressed because of gender. The African American church, with its current intoxication with the pursuit of wealth and creature comforts, is being compassionately warned to preach the gospel. That gospel demands liberation for all people regardless of gender.

Many male pastors and preachers would strengthen their preaching in immeasurable ways if they were to make a serious commitment to understanding the feminist and womanist theological perspectives. Over the years many male pastors have experienced a sense of insecurity after hearing the feminist alarm calling women congregants to fight for freedom from male domination and to distance themselves from patriarchal religious traditions. There is a clear need for a preaching methodology that allows for the liberation of male *and* female as they sit in the pews and listen to the sermonic presentation.

Dr. Flake really lives in ministry as a player-coach. The pain of her own ministry upbringing and her struggles against traditional theologies both serve to qualify her in that role. She is sensitive to the male and female coexistence that must be present in the African American church. She embodies such coexistence in the healthy copastoring model she has forged at Greater Allen. In her ministry, she has proven that you can be a true womanist theologian without creating an adversarial role with male church leadership. Her preaching methods are important for any pastor who is attempting to provide an atmosphere for the spiritual growth of both men and women. Her sermons are powerful frameworks from which preachers can glean how to do it right.

The African American church has to model God's imagination for God's creation. Dr. Flake has found a way to articulate that call and show us the way. I pray that her words of challenge and healing will find a deep place in preachers' sermonic thought and practice.

—Rev. Dr. William H. Curtis
President, 2007–10
Hampton University Ministers'
and Musicians' Conference
Senior Pastor
Mt. Ararat Baptist Church
Pittsburgh, Pennsylvania

Acknowledgments

No work is an isolated effort. The support, talents, and sacrifices of several have combined to help produce this project.

I am greatly indebted to the prolific womanist writers and lecturers who introduced me to and helped cultivate my own womanist perspectives. Their faithfulness to themselves and to all African American women is inspiring and empowering, and has been the very foundation of this writing. And my gratitude goes to the myriad black preachers whose creativity and prophetic insights have shown me new dimensions of biblical interpretation and preaching. My good friend Renita Jean Weems, who is a profound combination of womanist scholar and preacher, has been a special inspiration to me, as have female preachers across this country who have been courageous enough to uncover our stories in the biblical text.

My husband, Floyd, and my children, Aliya, Nailah, Rasheed, and Hasan, are five of God's greatest gifts to me, and their love and support have provided me the time and peace of mind needed to complete this work. They gave me the encouragement and "space" that I so desperately needed. Finally, my thanks also goes to the women (and men) of the congregation of the Greater Allen African Methodist Episcopal Cathedral.

My Journey to a Womanist Theology

My faith journey began at the St. Jude Missionary Baptist Church in Memphis, Tennessee, where my mother and I and all of my maternal relatives were very active members. In our church, as in most Southern black churches, there was a strong emphasis on the "conversion" experience. To ensure a safe journey through puberty, it was expected that this experience occur at the age of twelve, which was believed to be the "age of accountability." My mother, a Memphis school teacher, concluded that I was way too precocious, or "womanish" (a term to describe headstrong African American girls), to wait until age twelve. Thus, at the tender age of nine, Momma dragged me to the "mourner's bench" (the physical place where the conversion experience was believed to take place), and during the first night of our annual revival, I joined the ranks of the "born again."

Participation in Sunday school, the Baptist Training Union, and the youth choir were all a part of my church experience. It was there that I learned the skills of memorization and oratory, which have helped me to develop many of the gifts that I use today. In my early church experience, however, it was the preaching moment during worship that I remember best and that fascinated me the most. I was intrigued by the preacher's energy and rhythmic cadence. The unique manifestations of the Holy Spirit excited me as did the effect that preaching had on many members of the congregation. The joy and comfort that resulted from hearing the preaching of the gospel seemed almost mystical. In spite of all that was bad in people's lives in the segregated South, the soulful articulation of the gospel through God's preacher seemed to make the bad tolerable.

Sermons, as were all of the teaching and traditions of my early religious upbringing, were based on a strict and fundamentalist biblical interpretation. This was true particularly with respect to the roles and expectations of women. For instance, I grew up believing that the Bible forbade a woman to wear pants, to enter the church with her head uncovered, even to play cards. With respect to women's roles in the church, St. Jude's church meetings typically began with the reading of 1 Corinthians 14:34: "Let your women keep silence in the churches: for it is not permitted unto them to speak" (KJV). The historical and cultural context in which Paul writes and the soundness of the doctrine espoused therein were never discussed or challenged. Naturally, the notion of a female preacher was never entertained in my little church. Indeed, my grandfather, a leading trustee, believed that God never intended for women to become preachers or to hold any other leadership position in the church.

My initial "God experience" emerged within this cultural context. I accepted what I was taught about the role of women in the life of the church and did not know what it meant to question or explore deeper meaning within the biblical text. I do not believe that my experience was uncommon then, nor is it today. I would venture to say that many churchgoers continue to take 1 Corinthians 14:34 at face value, even believing that questioning or challenging traditional interpretations is akin to blasphemy.

As this "womanish" girl became a young woman, my perspective about the role of the church and the role of women therein began to change. As a student at Fisk Institute in Nashville, Tennessee, in the 1960s, I was first exposed to African American preachers such as James Cone and Gayraud Wilmore. These preachers and others challenged the black church to recognize God as a God of liberation and Jesus as an advocate for the oppressed, the poor, and the unwanted. As a result, I began to view the church as an institution whose role was to serve as a liberating force in the lives of individuals and the community.

During graduate school, my "God experience" deepened even further when I united with St. Paul A.M.E. Church in Cambridge, Massachusetts. It was there that I was exposed to a "nonliteral" interpretation of the biblical text as well as to biblical scholarship as a discipline. As I uncovered historical information from various biblical commentaries, I found new meaning in Scripture and began to abandon many of the misconstrued teachings of my childhood.

It was also in Cambridge that I first heard the voice of a female preacher. Seeing a woman stand behind a pulpit and hearing her preach felt very natural even though it was a completely foreign experience. I gained a new perspective on myself and on my potential in the life of the church, and I recognized that women could be called and chosen to enter the ministry just as men. While this woman preacher's mere presence was affirming, her nonsexist biblical interpretation and dynamic delivery combined to produce a sermon about the women at the tomb on the day of Jesus' resurrection that was both stirring and penetrating. I cried for a week.

From that point on, I began to search Scripture for a special "word" for women. I looked with special interest to stories about women found in the four Gospels. I paid particular attention to the stories whose themes were relevant to the lives of African American women. What began as a fascination soon turned into the mission around which my ministry has centered. I did not accept the call to ministry until several years later; however, this experience served as a foundation for my being open to the call. The "womanish" little girl from St. Jude's Baptist Church became a "womanist" preacher and teacher committed to assuring that every woman, especially African American women, finds God in her midst.

Introduction

For more than thirty years, my husband, Floyd, and I have served together in ministry at Allen A.M.E. Church in Queens, New York. We currently serve in the role of copastors. During our tenure, I have been very intentional about ministering to wounded women. The apostle Paul taught that transformation begins with the renewing of the mind. Thus, serving as a catalyst for God's healing has required the challenging of traditional biblical interpretations and the retelling of biblical stories in ways that affirm women and embrace unconventional points of view. While workshops, retreats, and conferences serve as vehicles through which ministry liberates the hearts and minds of hurting women, the worship experience, particularly the preaching moment, serves as the foundation from which emotionally and spiritually transforming messages emerge.

Songs may fill the sanctuary and prayers may touch people's hearts, but no moment is more vital to the worship experience than the preached Word. The sermon or homily is the essence of the church's link with the almighty God. Those who attend worship come with various problems, concerns, and expectations. Worshipers come needing and hoping for a word from the Lord. They come not only hoping that the word will make the bad tolerable but also that their lives will be transformed.

Responsibility and integrity demand, therefore, that the preached word is both salvific and liberating to all people. While "black preaching" has traditionally demonstrated a commitment to the eradication of sin and the liberation of the African American community from racism, social injustice, and economic oppression, by and large, it has not included elements that are sensitive to the experiences of African American women. If anything, preaching in the black church has tended to include biblical interpretations that have robbed women of their freedom and authentic personhood. Indeed, some interpretations have accommodated, even perpetuated, African American women's oppression and sense of woundedness.

Similarly, preaching that embraces a feminist theological perspective has promoted the eradication of sexism and gender bias in biblical interpretation and preaching (the use of gender-inclusive language being a significant contribution). However, feminist analysis has tended to focus solely on gender issues without communicating or reflecting African American women's cultural realities and their experiences with racism, sexism, and classism.

Womanist theology emerged as an expression of the dissatisfaction of a large number of African American women with the way the power arrangements of society and the feminist and black liberation responses thereto did not adequately respond to their issues or give voice to their unique perspective and experiences. A womanist perspective on preaching maintains that if the preached word is to serve its salvific and liberating purposes for all people, African American women's experiences and perspective must be acknowledged and included. If preaching is to truly reach the hearts, minds, and souls of African American women, preachers must employ an analysis of Scripture that reconstructs the Word of God in ways that are liberating to women as well as men and that reflects the totality of the African American experience.

Sermon development should depart from traditional, solely male-centered interests and perspectives. First and foremost, preaching must acknowledge sexism and racism as dual realities operating in the lives of African American women and be intentional about including sermonic elements that speak to those realities.

The primary aim of this book is to provide a theological paradigm that will enable preachers and other church leaders, both women and men, to understand and fulfill their responsibility to preach liberation and empowerment to marginalized and hurting African American women. The work is concerned with various practical applications of the theories and perspectives embraced in womanist theology. It is my hope that this book will help move the church, particularly the black church, to a greater understanding of the importance of embracing biblical interpretations and preaching methodologies that respond to and affirm the perspectives and experiences of African American women. It is my further hope that in doing so the church will be better equipped to serve as a source of healing for African American women.

Chapter 1 examines a major source of pain for African American women—experiences with physical and sexual violence. Chapter 2 contains a brief discussion of the development of womanist theology as a response to the shortcoming of black liberation and feminist theology. Chapter 3 suggests methodologies and practical considerations that can be employed in interpreting Scripture and presenting messages that provide a source of healing for African American women. Chapter 4 takes a new look at three misunderstood women of the Bible—Job's wife, Hagar, and the woman with an issue of blood—and affirms the kinship between their experiences and the experiences of African American women. The remaining chapters are composed of sermons that provide examples of the methodologies discussed in chapter 3.

PART 1

A Womanist Hermenuetic of Healing

1

Perspective on Pain

Pain is a reality in all of our lives. Whether it is the physical pain of illness or the emotional and spiritual pain of losing a loved one, all human beings have painful experiences. In fact, under some circumstances we even invite painful experiences on ourselves as a way of reaching a particular goal. The old adage "No pain, no gain," used most frequently within the physical fitness realm, expresses the notion that to obtain the goal of being fit and trim, one must endure the daily regimen of exercise even to the point of pain. Without question, in this life we all experience pain.

African American women have not cornered the market on pain. However, the pain we have suffered as a result of our race and ethnicity, God-given circumstances that we did not choose, has impacted our lives in profound ways. While African American women have endured numerous forms of oppression, including poverty and abandonment, perhaps the most ubiquitous form of oppression has resulted from our experience as victims of physical and sexual violence.

Since slavery, African American women have been subjected to physical and sexual violence. African slave women were vulnerable to rape and other forms of abuse that could only be inflicted on them because of gender. Sexual violence against black women slaves was not the slaveholder's expression of sexual lust as is sometimes assumed. Rather, the sexual violence was an expression of the slaveholders' quest for power and control over the slaves. It was a means of keeping slave women in their places—submissive, subservient, oppressed, and repressed. The dehumanizing and systematic violence against women during slavery laid the foundation for the sexual objectification of African American women and has also colored the response to the continued violence that some African American women experience today.

Current statistics show that African American women experience high rates of both physical and sexual violence. Unlike slavery, much of this violence is perpetuated by African American men. United States Department of Justice statistics indicate that African American women experience violence at disproportionate levels.[1] African American women have the highest rate of intimate violence, which is violence perpetrated by a spouse, former spouse, or boyfriend of any ethnic group, and are three times more likely than white women to die at the hands of an intimate partner.[2] African American women also report a higher rate of sexual violence. In a survey of high school students cited by the Centers for Disease Control's (CDC), National Center for Injury Prevention and Control, African American female students reported the highest incidence of forced sexual intercourse among all ethnic groups.[3] The CDC also reported that women of color are more likely to report being raped than white women. Without question, violence is a reality in the lives of a disproportionate number of African American women, as is the resulting spiritual and emotional trauma.

Research has found that African American women "are particularly likely to use religious coping strategies and are more likely to seek help from a minister than from any other helping professional."[4] In some cases, however, religious views have negatively affected African American women's perception of their experience with violence as well as their willingness to seek treatment. A key finding in a study that surveyed attitudes about domestic violence in the African American community found that religious beliefs caused some African American women to be less willing to disclose domestic violence. The beliefs that "God will take care of it" and "pray and the Lord will change him" were expressed as reasons for keeping violence a secret.[5]

Despite African American women's likelihood to turn to the church for help in crises that involve violence, many African American preachers have been unforgivably silent about condemning expressions of violence against women. Instead, there has been a tendency to restrict the parameters of racism and sexism to discussions of economic exploitation, equal employment opportunities, political injustices, stereotyping, and social stratification with respect to race, class, and gender. Even worse, pulpits have been largely occupied with preachers who deny the existence of misogyny and the patriarchal underpinnings of violence against women. Some voices have even degraded women by espousing a "blame-the-victim" theology. As a result, the pain and woundedness of female victims of male violence have been compounded by a sense of guilt and humiliation.

An outgrowth of the aforementioned mentality has led some pastors and other church leaders to counsel victims of violence to "Go home, obey your husband, and everything will be all right." Even those who may not have been told so directly may infer from traditional biblical interpretations regarding gender roles that Scripture requires them to do so. I recently heard the story of a woman who endured spousal abuse because she did not believe that her being beaten was a ground for divorce in God's eyes.

Rev. Al Miles, a Church of God minister and domestic violence prevention advocate argues in his book *Domestic Violence: What Every Pastor Needs to Know* that clergy in general have hindered rather than helped victims of domestic violence: "Our apathy, denial, exhortations, ignorance, misinterpretation of the Bible have added to women's pain and suffering and placed them in even greater danger....[Clergy] have the responsibility to preach and teach the biblical truth of God's love which binds women and men together as equals rather than ordering them in a hierarchy."[6]

Helping African American women heal from the pain of violence requires intervention on multiple levels, including the mental health and criminal justice systems. The church has a responsibility to steer women toward a variety of systems for assistance. However, as "keepers of their souls," we are responsible for sending messages that transform a culture of violence into a culture of healing. Preaching healing to African American women who have experienced the pain of violence must challenge the notion that violence against women is in any way justified. It must also move into the hurting places of the female community by naming the sins of their male perpetrators and dismantling all antifemale attitudes, even those perpetuated in Scripture. Moreover, messages for victims of violence must alleviate guilt, blame, and shame; minister healing to their wounded hearts, minds, and spirits; and empower them to lead fulfilled and productive lives.

NOTES

1. Department of Justice, *Criminal Victimization 2004*, Washington: Government Printing Office, 2006, no. NCJ 213257, www.ojp.usdoj.gov/bjs/pub/pdf/cvus/current/cvo401.pdf.

2. Department of Justice, *Violence by Intimates*, Washington: Government Printing Office, 1998, no. NCJ 167237, www.ojp.usdoj.gov/bjs/pub/pdf/vi.pdf.

3. Centers for Disease Control and Prevention, *Sexual Violence Fact Sheet*, www.cdc.gov/ncipc/factsheets/svfacts.htm.

4. Carl C. Bell and Jacqueline Mattis, *The Importance of Cultural Competence in Ministering to African American Victims of Domestic Violence*, History of the Institute on Domestic Violence in the African American Community, 1999, www.dvinstitute.org/Proceedings/1999/1999_part2.pdf.

5. Vetta S. Thompson, and Anita Bazile, *African American Attitudes toward Domestic Violence and DV Assistance*, National Violence Against Women Prevention Research Center, 2000, www.vawprevention.org/research/attititudesdv.shtml.

6. Al Miles, *Domestic Violence: What Every Pastor Needs to Know* (Minneapolis: Augsburg Fortress, 2000). Quoted on www.faithtrustinstitute.org.

2

Womanist Theological Roots

Because preaching healing to wounded women is rooted in a womanist theological perspective, this section will briefly explore the roots of womanist theology and its emergence as a response to the shortcomings of black liberation and feminist theologies.

Having shared the same African heritage, the same slave ships, the same cotton fields, and the same segregated water fountains, the mutual oppression and suffering in racist America should have created such a bond between African American women and men that sexism would not have been a reality within our community. Yet one of the most painful realities that African American women in America have had to suffer has been oppression at the hand of our "brothers." Because African American men rejected the racism of the patriarchal structures of America, it was difficult for African American women to understand how their "cosufferers" could continue to embrace the white patriarchal model of female oppression. Yet as some African American men gained participation and power in white, male-dominated America, they used that power to subjugate the same women with whom they had partnered in the struggle for racial equality.

Initially, African American women as a whole were publicly silent about African American men's sexism, not because they did not desire to end their maltreatment, but because they felt that the most important issue was liberation from racist oppression. As time passed, however, African American women's experiences with subtle and overt gender oppression within the African American community were so glaringly akin to patriarchal oppression that African American women could not continue to suppress their hurt and indignation. The same thirst for human dignity that made them speak out against the injustices of racism also compelled them to end their silence about sexist treatment at the hands of African American men.

African American women hoped that their call for equality would heighten the consciousness of African American men and challenge them to abandon their sexist behavior. By and large, that did not happen even in seminaries. James Cone writes that when the issue of African American male sexism was first raised by African American women at Union Theological Seminary in New York City and other places, African American men did not take seriously African American women's concern. Rather, the men continued to accept the illusion that "African American women have always been free."[1]

African American men's definition of "freedom" clearly meant freedom from racism for African American men. Even though they talked about human equality as they struggled for freedom from racism, many adopted their oppressors' patriarchal structures and embraced the notion of male supremacy and domination. Ironically, they allowed the same traditions that preserved black enslavement, colonialism, and imperialism to provide the normative perception of women for the African American community. African American men allowed the "enemy" to define the realities of the African American woman in their own communities, and they perpetuated the same oppression they claimed to abhor.

The theology that emerged from the black liberation movement reflected the same gender bias as the movement itself. When African American women realized that their freedom was not a priority in the fight for liberation, they were compelled to challenge their male counterparts on theological issues. Jacquelyn Grant, who made one of the earliest critiques of black liberation theology's exclusion of the experiences of African American women, writes: "It is difficult to understand how Black men manage to exclude the liberation of Black women from their interpretation of the liberating gospel. Any correct analysis of the poor and oppressed would reveal some interesting and inescapable facts about the situation of women within oppressed groups."[2]

If black liberation thinking was authentic and grounded in a liberating anthropology and theology, inherent in that tradition would be the affirmation that just as "in Christ there is neither slave nor free,

Jew nor Greek," likewise, "in Christ there is neither male nor female." Yet African American men as a whole had chosen to forget, overlook, and deny that the same Bible that rejects racism also rejects sexism. African American women's liberation thinking envisioned a religio-socio-cultural system that fostered equality for all African American people—men, women, and children.

When many African American women saw that their "brothers" refused to take their cry for justice seriously, they could no longer completely reject the white feminist movement from which they had remained apart. No longer could they assert that the struggle for women's rights was solely a white middle-class phenomenon that was unrelated to the African American community's liberation movement. African American women were forced to question and challenge the African American man's commitment to the black liberation struggle, in light of his conscious oppression of African American women. Some African American women began to embrace feminist theology.

Initially, African American female theologians who embraced feminist theology were known as "black feminists." Their experiences with sexism, both inside and outside their community, forced African American women of the seventies to try to identify with white women's experiences with sexist oppression. They attempted to move in feminist liberation circles, just as their nineteenth-century ancestors had affiliated with the women's suffrage movement. However, it became obvious to African American women that the feminist movement, like its predecessor, generally excluded nonwhite women. The feminist movement was narrowly defined by white women; its ideologies and traditions were grounded solely in white women's history and experiences.

White women's analysis of the women's oppression did not appropriately communicate or honestly reflect African American women's cultural realities and experiences with sexism, racism, and classism. Not only was the full breadth of the African American women's oppression excluded, but their oppression was inadequately defined. Womanist theologian Delores Williams claims that the experience of African American females is misrepresented when their oppression is expressed in terms of a language that only identifies men as oppressors of women.[3] To define *patriarchy* as "rule by men," and to name it as the structure that is responsible for the oppression of all women, denies the role that white women have chosen as oppressors of women. While patriarchy may describe the white feminists' oppression, it is also the institution that has designed and encouraged their oppression of African American women. Hence, a nomenclature that named patriarchy as the evil that oppresses all women was inadequate for the naming of the control and subjugation of African American women by white males *and* females.

Similarly, feminist theology, which only named sexism as a source of oppression in the church, ignored the reality of racism and classism that also plagues the church. To be sure, African American women acknowledged and abhorred the existence of sexism inside and outside the academies and the Christian church. While African American women were the victims of sexist institutions and acts perpetrated by both European American and African American men, to embark on a one-dimensional theological intent would have been self-injurious and "short-visioned." African American women's theology needed to confront the full gamut of sins that oppressed them and their community.

Another shortcoming of feminist theology is its failure to reflect the African American women's love of the Holy Spirit and the respect shown for the presence and the work of the Holy Spirit. The white feminist emphasis on language, liturgy, and symbolism used in the worship experience is secondary for many African American women. For many African American women, the first desire is that the Spirit move in worship in ways that minister healing and liberation to the entire church community. Likewise, Jacquelyn Grant rightly contends that feminists have failed to deal with the black women's Jesus as Jesus has been revealed to and experienced by African American women.[4] White women theologians have been so preoccupied with the maleness of Jesus that they have essentially scorned black women's understanding of the significance of Jesus and their comfort with his gender. For the African American woman, it is the humanity of Christ, the reality of his experiences with oppression, and his ultimate victory over that oppression with which she identifies.

In response to the oversights of the black liberation and feminist theology movements, African American women developed a theology that called for a holistic healing and redemption of the African American community, the church, the academies, and society. Womanist theology emerged from the African American community and experience. Its path of development has been from the community into the academy. Its presence in the academy and its emergence as a viable "theology" is clearly owed to the expressed dissatisfaction of a large number of African American women, inside and outside the academy, with the power arrangements of society. Womanist theologians resented the lack of integrity that characterized the traditions of their so-called advocates, and brought forth a privatized theology that rejected the African American woman's traditionally assigned roles in society and within the African American community. Their experience as wives, lovers, mothers, and sisters was so significant, however, that their fight for liberation and deliverance from all oppressive structures could not be to the exclusion of the African American family. The knowledge that European American families in every social class have the power to oppress the African American family dictated that the goals for African American women's liberation could not be separated from her desire for her family's liberation. Even the reality of black-male-oppression could not distract African American women from their commitment to the liberation of African American men. Theirs would, indeed, be a universal effort to raise the consciousness of the whole of humanity with regard to gender, race and class oppression.

Womanist theologians span the socioeconomic, political, and educational gamut of the African American Christian community. Their theology is expressed in the language of women who are committed to the validation of the African American experience in society, religion, and history. Every womanist theologian is a *mother*, for though she may or may not have borne a child, she nurtures all African American people in the liberation struggle. She is a *contemporary prophet*, calling forth other women to break away from the oppressive ideologies and belief systems that presume to define their reality. She is *preacher*, *teacher*, and *student*, who takes seriously her responsibility to discover truth and articulate it in a language that guarantees and strengthens her own self-importance and that of her community. She loves herself and her Jesus, and she knows that God is a spirit who is free of gender and racial designation. She is empowered by the knowledge that she knows best how to fight for her own liberation and the liberation of her people, and she is committed to doing so. African American Christian women's gift to themselves, their community, and humankind is womanist theology. As African American women develop and expand, womanist theology will develop and expand, and together they will create and discover new dimensions of personhood, worship experiences, and life in their community.

NOTES

1. James Cone, *My Soul Looks Back* (Nashville: Abingdon, 1992), 118.

2. Jacquelyn Grant, *Black Theology and the Black Woman*, Black Theology: A Documentary History, Volume One: 1966–1979 (Maryknoll, NY: Orbis Books, 1979), 123.

3. Delores Williams, "The Color of Feminism: Or Speaking the Black Woman's Tongue," *Journal of Religious Thought* 43, no. 1 (Spring–Summer 1986).

4. Jacquelyn Grant, *White Women's Christ and Black Women's Jesus* (Atlanta: Scholars Press, 1989), 200.

3

Preaching to Heal

Preachers, both male and female, must be committed to the spiritual and emotional health of African American women. They should consistently read Scripture to discover new interpretive strategies that will expose and denounce the horrors of race and gender oppression and equip the entire congregation with spiritual and pragmatic strategies that will empower and heal. No longer can those who are called to the office of preacher embrace biblical interpretations that ignore or contribute to African American women's mental and emotional oppression and woundedness.

Recognizing and acknowledging the various sources of pain for African American women is an important first step toward the church becoming a source for healing. The wounds inflicted by unhappy, love-deficient marriages or relationships; the frustration and loneliness that accompany divorce and single parenting; and the life-altering impact of crime, alcoholism, drug abuse, incest, and rape affect the emotional state of many women within a congregation. As a result, self-hatred, guilt, depression, anxiety, and emotional instability are evils that attack women in communities of faith. The church must offer hope for renewal and commitment to the overall health and well-being of women in pain. The preaching moment should not reflect an appropriation of the views and philosophies of the flagrant or subtle oppression within our culture. Rather, at the heart of the gospel message is the call to transformation and renewal.

For the preached word, in particular, to become a source for healing, those who bring a word from the Lord Sunday after Sunday, week after week, and year after year must employ careful and compassionate

scriptural interpretation, preaching methodologies, and overall practices that provide the appropriate salve.

Interpretive Methods

The following section presents five methodologies of scriptural interpretation recommended to preachers for presenting sermons that
effectively minister to hurting women. Moreover, it deals with some
practices and pitfalls to avoid when preaching to restore the hearts and
minds of wounded women.

Affirm

> Whatever is true, whatever is honorable, whatever is
> just, whatever is pure, whatever is pleasing, whatever
> is commendable, if there is any excellence, and if there
> is anything worthy of praise, think about these things.
> —Philippians 4:8

In sermonic settings, rarely are texts used in ways that affirm
women's perspectives and experiences. Probably the first expo-
sure that many of us, preachers and laypersons alike, had to biblical texts that involve female characters was negative. We heard
that Eve was responsible for the fall of humankind. We heard sermons that chastised Job's wife for her blasphemous outburst in
response to her husband's plight. If the woman at the well from
John 4 was mentioned, typically it was to highlight her multiple
marriages and the fact that when she met Jesus she had a live-in
boyfriend. And all of us heard sermons about the conniving antics
of Jezebel and Delilah.

Affirming the positive role that women played and continue to play
in shaping our faith is a vital tool in the healing process. A wounded
woman who already feels bad about herself does not need to be further wounded by the perception that in the eyes of Scripture, and
therefore in the eyes of God, she is innately evil or beyond redemption.
Traditional perspectives and notions about biblical women must
therefore be turned on their heads. Preachers must rethink and

reshape stories of biblical women in ways that uplift and remove the taint of traditional interpretations.

For example, an affirming look at Eve recognizes her role as the mother of all creation. An affirming view of Job's wife acknowledges her as a cosufferer with Job as opposed to demonizing her for a momentary faith lapse. An affirming examination of the woman at the well focuses not on the number of husbands she had, but instead on the number of people she brought to Christ after her encounter with the Savior. An affirming word is a healing word.

Show Sensitivity
Traditional biblical interpretations have tended to judge biblical women in insensitive ways. There has been a failure overall to consider the totality of the circumstances that may have given rise to the woman's action or perspective. In the story of Job, for example, the author views the plight of the family solely through Job's eyes. There is no acknowledgment that Job's wife also suffered as a result of the losses the family experienced. There is utter failure both within the text and historically to discuss her suffering. Thus, it has been easy for anyone interpreting the text to demonize her completely for a momentary faith lapse.

Similarly, the unique circumstances and perspectives of African American women are often ignored in traditional and even contemporary theological paradigms. Feminist theological methodologies have typically ignored race, while black liberation theology has generally ignored gender. Consequently, the emergent preaching methodologies of those theologies are not sensitive to the contextual reality of being both African American and female. Race and gender oppression are interrelated realities for African American women, operating in tandem in their everyday lives. Interpretation of the biblical text must be sensitive to all circumstances, past and present, that affect the lives and that color the perspective of African American women.

Preaching methodologies must be sensitive to the full spectrum of life circumstances, including the perspective of African American women. Such sensitivity allows the preached word to fully embody Isaiah's mission as carried out in the ministry of Jesus Christ:

The Spirit of the Lord GOD is upon me,
    because the LORD has anointed me;
he has sent me to bring good news to the oppressed,
    to bind up the brokenhearted,
to proclaim liberty to the captives,
    and release to the prisoners; …
    to comfort all who mourn…
to provide for those who mourn in Zion—
    to give them a garland instead of ashes,
the oil of gladness instead of mourning,
    the mantle of praise instead of a faint spirit.
                                    —Isaiah 61:1-3

Honor Tradition

I am reminded of your sincere faith, a faith that dwelt first in your grandmother Lois and your mother Eunice and now, I am sure, dwells in you as well.
                                    —2 Timothy 1:5

African American cultural traditions are deeply rooted in the Christian faith. From the Middle Passage through segregation, when African Americans had nothing else, we had our God, our Jesus, and our church. It is necessary, therefore, in reshaping traditions that have oppressed women, that we not, as an ancient German proverb states, "throw out the baby with the bath water."

In reconceptualizing traditional biblical interpretations that have undergirded preaching in ways that affirm and show sensitivity to African American women's experiences, care must be taken that the emergent preaching is not stripped of traditional elements that are a source of comfort and liberation for African American women. Remember, one of womanist theology's criticisms of feminist theology is its tendency to redefine elements that are central to many African American women's understanding of who God is.

The Psalms have been a source of inspiration and comfort to African American women for generations. When highlighting, therefore, the role that David played in the oppression of his wife Michal, care must be taken not to "demonize" David, the psalmist, in ways that undermine completely his contribution to the tradition of faith embraced by many African American women and their fore-mothers. Maintaining African American women's desire to cleave to religious and cultural traditions that helped us "get over" is necessary even as we seek to challenge and eradicate those traditions that are oppressive.

Liberate

In addition to the need for preachers to affirm women's perspectives, show sensitivity to the unique experiences of black women, and honor African American cultural traditions, the Word of God must be interpreted and presented as a voice of liberation for all people. African American people found liberation in Scripture even during a time when European slaveholders interpreted Scripture to justify the institution of slavery in America. The liberating essence of the Bible provided enslaved African American Christian women with a God-reality that supported their struggle to achieve authentic human existence. This understanding of the nature of God inspired them to use an interpretive process and methodology that spoke to their experiences.

Jarena Lee, the first woman to be licensed to preach in the A.M.E. Church, and Sojourner Truth, abolitionist and an advocate for voting rights for women, are examples of women whose faith served as a catalyst for confronting both racial and gender injustices. They viewed God as a liberating force in their lives and the lives of the people for whom they struggled.

Preaching a liberating word to women also requires that traditional biblical interpretations that have removed the teachings of Paul from their historical and cultural context as a way of silencing women in the church be challenged and retaught. Preaching that responds to the evils of racial discrimination but turns a blind eye to gender discrimination must be confronted for its hypocrisy. Christ came to free all oppressed people, women as well as men. Liberating preaching must do so as well.

Present Jesus as an Advocate for Women

Throughout his ministry, Jesus defended women whom others in the culture "put down." The woman caught in the act of adultery, the woman who anointed Jesus' feet with oil, and the Samaritan woman so ostracized that she was forced to draw water at the well in the heat of the day are but a few examples of stories in which Jesus challenged the status quo with respect to women.

For African American women in pain, the story of the woman with an infirmity in the Gospel of Luke in particular evinces Jesus' unquestionable and uncompromising concern for women. As this bent-over, spirit-oppressed woman entered the synagogue on the Sabbath, Jesus was touched with compassion for her and moved in such a way that he healed her without any appeal from her to do so, and at the risk of incurring the wrath of his opponents. In this woman, African American women who are burdened and oppressed can see their experience with pain and emotional trauma as well as their deliverance from that oppression. Likewise, Jesus' encounter with the woman with the issue of blood further affirms Jesus' concern for wounded women, including African American women (Luke 8:43-48). The fact that Jesus pauses to minister to this woman in the midst of his dealings with an important man, Jarius (Luke 8:40-56), provides a message of healing to African American women who may feel invisible and ostracized.

Acknowledge African Ancestry

Traditional scriptural interpretations tend to glaze over the ancestry of biblical women of African descent. For example, Hagar, mother of Ishmael, was of Egyptian descent, and Zipporah, Moses' wife, was a Cushite (of Ethiopian descent), but both are traditionally relegated to the status of foreigners with little, if any, acknowledgment of their cultural heritage and its significance.

For African American women, Hagar is not merely Abraham's concubine. Rather, Hagar is a woman of color who symbolizes what it means to be used and cast away and yet who experienced the presence of God. Likewise, presentations of the story of Zipporah often neglect the reality that Miriam and Aaron hated their sister-in-law because she was black. Fully acknowledging the heritage and experiences of these women, rather than relegating their images to something less than their full personhood, is an affirming act for all women of color.

In addition, images that reflect the strength of women of African descent must also be highlighted. For example, Egyptian midwives exercised civil disobedience by refusing to kill the Hebrew baby boys as they had been instructed, and their story provides a testimony to the strength of African women who have stood against injustice (Exodus 1:15-22). It is important that African female imagery and the unique experiences and perspectives it represents are not masked as being insignificant or discounted as being unimportant. The ability to stand on the shoulders of strong biblical women of African descent helps to undergird the healing process. It affirms for wounded women of today, "If she could get through, so can I!"

Practical Considerations

In addition to the aforementioned methodologies, a number of important practical considerations are worth exploring with respect to preaching healing effectively to African American women. The following tips provide pragmatic and practical guidance to preachers.

Avoid Male-Bashing

Those who proclaim a holistic womanist interpretation of Scripture should avoid the tendency to present female-sensitive sermons that resort to male-bashing. At its best, womanist preaching embraces a paradigm that is integrative, ethical, and fair to men and women alike. Female-biased biblical interpretation is not the goal or the intent of womanist preaching. Those who preach should proclaim a gospel void of all gender-biased interpretation. The devaluation of African American men or any human being in order to affirm and heal African American women is antithetical to womanist preaching.

Moreover, any effort to exclude the African American male experience from the healing process would create a division within the church and community that would mitigate against communal solidarity. The black church must be unified in its fight against racism, oppression, and dehumanization. Consequently, preachers must avoid interpretations that create a context of contention and competition between men and women. Womanist theology and preaching derived from it supports the liberation of the whole African American community. One group cannot be affirmed or liberated at the expense of the other. A womanist analysis of Scripture must deconstruct traditional patriarchal interpretations and name and reject sins that are largely gender specific while not producing a discourse that is anti-male.

Tell the Truth

That said, a womanist interpretation cannot ignore, justify, or excuse the abusive and misogynist behavior of some African American men. The oppression and devaluation of men of color by white men may contribute to but by no means justifies spousal abuse, incest, family abandonment, or female objectification. The burdens that African American men endure are undeniable, but it only weakens and pollutes the strength of the church and community to allow silence to validate negative behavior. Any community can only be strengthened and elevated by a call to truth, integrity, and morality.

The truth sometimes hurts. Note that womanist interpretation of Scripture may offend men and women who resist or resent preaching that is grounded in historical and contextual truth and is based on an integrative and female-sensitive biblical interpretation. While truth and fairness can cause discomfort, it should not be viewed as oppressive or prejudicial. Responsible preachers must remain uncompromising to their call to preaching a holistic and liberating message. They must have an allegiance to the healing and salvation of the African American community as a whole.

Inspire Action

Most people listen to sermons from their own perspectives and experience. They are strengthened and affirmed most when a preacher employs strategies and interpretations that allow them to appropriate biblical stories and principles on a personal level. At the core of healing sermons, then, are a passion and truth that are a source of empowerment and a call to alter attitudes and actions. Sermons should motivate and inspire positive modification of thinking and behavior. That is one measure of a sermon's success.

Womanist preaching is, therefore, corrective and should elicit a positive, constructive, and life-changing response from the targeted community. It must not only proclaim the Word of God by communicating the healing contained therein, but the women and men who hear the gospel must perceive it as truth and be motivated to be "transformed by the renewing of [their] minds" (Romans 12:2) and actions. It should so inform, energize, reprove, and correct those who perceive it rightly and receive it fully that they will not be able to dismiss or repress it. Through the power of the Holy Spirit, preaching that is grounded in a womanist biblical interpretation has the potential to be so utterly penetrating and charismatic for those in the assembly that, to use Jeremiah's language, it will be like "fire shut up in [their] bones" (Jeremiah 20:9).

Think Outside the Box

Old habits die hard. Old ways of thinking die even harder. Eradicating traditional notions advanced by preaching that has underpinned and even contributed to African American women's oppression requires preachers to renew their own minds. Preachers will need resources that explore the nuances, causes, effects, and responses surrounding the pain of women. All preachers—even those who are themselves survivors of rape, incest, or abuse—should avail themselves of the vast body of literature that will broaden their knowledge and heighten their sensitivity to women's issues. They should appeal to books and articles that explore the religious roots of the rape, incest, and abuse of women, the psychological impact of these evils, and the role of the Christian church in addressing them. Women themselves are a primary source of information. Bible studies for women, private counseling sessions, one-on-one encounters, and even encounters at the altar will birth sensitivity to the need for addressing the pain of women through sermons.

Conclusion

Womanist preaching emphasizes survival and the reclaiming of self-esteem and dignity. It calls upon believers to draw from an inner strength and power that come from God. Insecurity, self-condemnation, and pessimism are named as sin, and the preacher calls for women and men alike to purge themselves of attitudes, behaviors, and perceptions that are self-destructive and self-defeating. A recurring theme of womanist preaching is that of God's power and passion to heal, liberate, and elevate all people above the trials and afflictions of the human experience. Just as the hymns, spirituals, and gospel music of the black church are largely expressions of human worth and testimonies of the resiliency of the believer's spirit, the premise and the practice of preaching should communicate the capacity to soar beyond experiences of oppression and woundedness.

4

A New Look at Misunderstood Women

The ability to show sensitivity toward and empathize with the circumstances in people's lives that may cause them to think or act in a particular way is the mark of a compassionate person. When preachers approach scriptural interpretation with care *and* compassion, they allow those who hear the Word to be touched in liberating and transforming ways. Therefore, it is essential for preachers to examine from an empathetic and sensitive perspective the traditionally vilified or marginalized women in Scripture to shed new light on their oft-ignored suffering and the unfair judgments mounted against them.

Job's Wife (Job 2)

Buried in obscurity and anonymity, the name of Job's wife is withheld from us. She is an ignored and overlooked woman. The attention that is directed to her is essentially negative and full of condemnation. Little thought is given to her plight; little consideration is given to her losses. For years preachers have called her sinful and heretical and have compared her with Eve, Michal, Jezebel, and other female "villains" of the Bible. Few have viewed "Mrs. Job" as an individual, a cosufferer with her husband. Few have acknowledged her pain and despair. Instead, she has been callously condemned, convicted, and sentenced to the pages of history as a weak-minded, insensitive, and even evil woman.

To gain a different perspective on her plight, let us look at the life of Mrs. Job. The Bible says that her husband, Job, was a faithful man. Though it goes unsaid in Scripture, it is not far-fetched to believe that Mrs. Job was a faithful woman. *They* had seven sons and three daughters. *They* had thousands of sheep and camels, hundreds of sheep and donkeys. *They* lived in a large house with a large number of servants. *They* were two very wealthy people. Because Job is described as the greatest man in the kingdom, we can believe that Job's wife was the greatest woman in the kingdom.

The biblical text records that one day disaster struck. Their cattle were destroyed, their sheep were killed, their servants and their finances were gone. To add injury to insult, after losing everything they owned, they received the devastating news that all ten of their children had been killed when a mighty wind crushed the house down upon them.

Biblical scholars and theologians refer to this tragedy as "Job's test." But clearly this was "Mrs. Job's test," too. Anyone who has ever been married knows that when "two become one," there is no pain that one feels that the other does not feel. Yet the biblical camera focuses only on Mr. Job, providing us with a picture of his sorrow and his grief. Though it seems obvious that Job's wife suffered along with her husband, we are left without a picture of what she experienced as a result of the tragedy.

Off in a corner somewhere was the mother of those children, heart breaking, head spinning, body feeling crushed by the mountain of misery that had fallen in on her. The fruit of her womb, the children she had borne, loved, and nurtured were dead. Mrs. Job's world had been destroyed by the "heavenly wager" that had been designated for her husband. The pain only intensified for this woman when her husband was stricken with a horrible disease that produced sores and boils all over his body. Imagine what it must have been like for Mrs. Job—her earthly possessions gone, her children dead, and her husband pitifully sick. How much more could a woman take?

Then, in the midst of the trauma, Mrs. Job finds her afflicted husband sitting on a dunghill among ashes in so much physical and emotional anguish that he held a sharp, ragged-edged piece of pottery in his hand that he used to scrape and lacerate his severely inflamed body. This piteous and grievous sight must have sent Mrs. Job "over the edge." While Job's physical pain was not her physical reality, having to experience vicariously the demise and pain of her husband was sure to have caused Mrs. Job mental and emotional trauma. Though her physical body was intact, her mind and spirit were being destroyed. It would have been difficult for such a tormented woman to proclaim the goodness of God in the midst of innocent and "undeserved" suffering. It should be no surprise that in all of her pain and brokenness, Mrs. Job experienced moments in which her faith faltered. At one such moment, she cried out to Job, "Do you still persist in your integrity? Curse God, and die" (Job 2:9).

These words have provoked commentators, past and present, to scorn Mrs. Job. Just as Job did not understand his wife's anguish and spoke disparagingly of her, generations of men and women have followed his lead. Yet any woman who has experienced great loss and intense pain should be able to relate to Mrs. Job's outburst. She saw Job's agony and experienced her own. Anger and frustration had overtaken her. She may have suggested death as a solution to Job's suffering because she wished death herself. Her misery was so great that faith and courage were unattainable at that moment. One might even conjecture that Mrs. Job's audible outburst was accompanied by a secret prayer for salvation and restoration that history could not record.

This woman's human reaction to her husband and her God has for centuries been said to defy all notions of proper female behavior and spiritual propriety and flies in the face of traditional thinking about what it means to be faithful. Euthanasia and apostasy are deemed theologically offensive even under the worst circumstances. Yet Job's wife's words of despair are a foreshadowing of Job's similar words in later chapters. Job's wife recognizes long before Job what is at stake theologically when the faithful suffer innocently. She brings to bear the conflict between innocence and integrity on the one hand and an affirmation of the goodness of God on the other. Yet traditional biblical interpretation disregards the reality of Mrs. Job's suffering in ways that typify patriarchal injustice.

A sensitive reading does not discount or minimize Mrs. Job's experience. Rather, it sees her as the prototype of female social and religious nonconformists who challenge traditional views of God and the world. She is every woman who has been bold enough to question the move of God. Her questions reflect a pathos and dignity that only a woman who has hopelessly sought to provide healing for her broken family would understand.

African American women can uniquely relate to the experience of Job's wife. We can see in her character doubt and frustration similar to what we experience in our lives. Historically, we have had our babies snatched from our breasts, our children shot down in the streets, our husbands debilitated by various physical and social conditions. We can identify with this woman's losses and agony. If truth be told, her moments of faithlessness were no greater than the moments of faithlessness and despair that we have experienced ourselves.

A superficial reading of the book of Job has caused many African American preachers to identify with Job as a hero and to reject his wife. Job's suffering, his faith and patience, and his ultimate restoration have traditionally spoken to the experience and hope of African American people. An interpretation that is sensitive to the struggles of African American women, however, suggests that Job's wife represents our experience with utter sorrow, poverty, humiliation, and misunderstanding in this country. Her restoration and doubled blessings in the final chapter of the book of Job remind us of God's tendency to redeem even the most unredeemable situations—in spite of our wavering faith. A womanist interpretation encourages African American women to relate to the experience of Job's wife and emphasizes the possibility of relief from suffering and hopelessness.

We cannot afford to judge Mrs. Job too quickly. For, if we look closely, we will see in this woman much of ourselves.

Hagar the Egyptian (Genesis 21:9-21)

Conventional interpretations of the Hagar story have provided a misleading characterization of this woman of African ancestry. Traditionally represented as the "silent" third adult member of the Abraham-Sarah household, her role within the household was defined as that of a slave-concubine. By virtue of her status and birth origin, she was viewed as inferior to Sarai and Abram. Her objectification by her two superiors creates an image of an oppressed and tragic figure. Given to Abram as the channel through which the family would acquire an heir, Hagar was ultimately cast away. Hagar is a classic example of the mistreated and unprotected African American woman in an oppressive patriarchal society.

For centuries the African American community has appropriated the Hagar stories based on her blackness and her mistreatment as a woman and a slave. However, contemporary interpretations reveal that Hagar was more than a mere slave,—that there may have been something unique about her relationship with Sarai and her role in the family structure. Hagar was more than a victim of Sarai, a jealous, self-centered woman who would stop at nothing to achieve her own goals and accomplish her purposes, and a man, Abram, who ignored her personhood and her plight. Rather, Hagar was a woman of color whose God encounter resulted in triumph and complete restoration. Her oppression and subjugation remain one of the atrocities of biblical history. Yet a womanist perspective of the text reveals characteristics of this misunderstood woman that are worthy of affirmation.

Who was Hagar? When we first meet her, she is already a member of Abraham's household. She is described differently in the places within the text in which her story appears. In Genesis 16:1-16 she is called a *shiphchâh*; in Genesis 21:9-21 she is called an *'amah*. Both words portray her as one who is "owned" by Sarai and Abram. But how she came into their "possession" is unknown. Their association may have begun while Sarai and Abram were in Egypt (Genesis 12:10-20). Hebrew lore claims that Hagar was the daughter of the Egyptian pharaoh, who had been a gift from the pharaoh in whose palace Sarai resided.

The Hagar that we meet in 16:1-6 is a childless *shiphchâh*, or "maid," whom Sarai gives to Abram so that she might provide the childless couple with an heir. Because the word *shiphchâh* also means "virgin," it is likely that Hagar was a virgin when she was made to lie down with Abram. This indicates that Hagar had not been treated as the typical female slaves of that day who were commonly rented out (or treated) as concubines. Indeed, the two Hagar texts do not present any indication that Hagar functioned within the household as anything except one who bore a child. Thus, it is possible that she was brought into the household for the express purpose of functioning as a surrogate mother for Sarai's child.

When Hagar became pregnant, the text reveals that she began to "look with contempt on her mistress." This apparent attitude change caused Sarai to feel compelled to affirm her superior position to Hagar by dealing harshly with her. Humiliated and degraded, a proud Hagar rebelled and ran away from the household. Hagar's insensitive and abusive attitude toward an already hurting Sarai paints a rather negative picture of the *shiphchâh*, while Sarai emerges as a "victim" whose harsh treatment of Hagar is somewhat justified. Because of her role as progenitor, Hagar was viewed by Sarai as a threat and rival, and the "mistress" was pressed to put the "maid" in her place.

When the exploited Hagar ran away, she became the first female in biblical history to liberate herself from oppressive power structures. This act of self-assertion was not well viewed by Yahweh. An angel was dispatched to order Hagar back into the house of Abram. We will never know why God told Hagar to return to her mistress and submit to her (Genesis 16:9), but Hagar's response was an apparent indication of her willingness to submit to Yahweh's will. With no indication of anger, resentment, or doubt, Hagar immediately validated this divine encounter by naming God. "You are El-roi," she said "Have I really seen God and remained alive after seeing him?" (Genesis 16:13). In this wilderness experience, Hagar defies biblical tradition by receiving a covenant promise from Yahweh, an experience usually reserved for males, and by naming God—an authority that no other biblical figure assumed. Though the biblical text does not say, we assume that upon the departure of the divine messenger, Hagar returned home to await the birth of her son and the fulfillment of the promise.

The Hagar of chapter 21 is depicted more disparagingly than the Hagar of chapter 16. The tension between the two women intensifies as Sarai (now Sarah) has conceived and borne her husband, Abram (now Abraham), a son. Sarah no longer needs or wants Hagar or her son, Ishmael. Thus, at Sarah's behest, Hagar and her son are expelled from their household. While wandering thirsty in the hot desert, Hagar cried out in anguish about the condition of her son, whom she had cast under a bush. At last the storyteller grants Hagar some emotion.

If it is Hagar who cries, the narrator asserts that it is Ishmael whom God hears. In response to the child's voice, God reveals God's self to Hagar. God tells Hagar to "lift up the boy and hold him fast with your hand" (Genesis 21:18), stressing to her that she must never leave him again. She is all that he has. The words of God suggest a lifetime commitment to Hagar's son, as God promises life, land, and offspring.

Who is this Egyptian woman that she is visited by God twice? Why is she numbered with Abraham, Jacob, and Moses, the patriarchs to whom God appeared? Whatever the reason, because she is the first woman in Scripture to whom God directly appeared, Hagar is portrayed as the first genuine matriarch of the Old Testament, and she demonstrates that divine promise could be given to a woman, indeed to a woman of color and a non-Hebrew. Truly, God was with Hagar and ultimately participated in the liberation of this woman.

God's determination that Hagar would survive demonstrates to African American women God's concern for the survival of the African American community. Many African American women can identify with Hagar's circumstances, being used, cast away, and unable to make provision for our offspring. We have cried out in our despair. And even when no one else has heard us, God has. And God has appeared to us, giving us strength and courage to survive our desert experience, to move forward and create community.

Yes, to view Hagar as merely a slave/concubine or even a surrogate mother, is to misunderstand the true essence of the ways in which God has revealed and continues to reveal God's self to this misunderstood woman, and even to us.

A Desperate Woman (Mark 5:25-34; Luke 8:43-48)

Hopeless, frustrated, weak, weary, angry, lonely, depressed, desperate—all of these feelings and more could be used to describe just how she felt. For twelve seemingly endless years, this poor woman had suffered the tragedy of a broken body. For twelve long years she had been the victim of a condition or disorder that the Gospel writers, Mark and Luke, describe as "an issue of blood."

The woman with an issue of blood is perhaps the most preached about woman in the black church. Her story has been told from pulpits and lecterns across this country. She is discussed in workshops and on retreats. Even more than Mary, Esther, or Ruth, the designated female heroes of the Bible, this woman seems to capture our attention. Something about her makes us want to explore and relate to her human condition. She haunts our conscious and our subconscious realities. She has claimed her place in the "Christian Hall of Fame."

She is another nameless woman in Scripture. The writers simply call her the "the woman with the issue of blood." She is unique from other nameless women in the biblical text, such as the widow of Nain and Jarius's daughter, who are identified according to their male kinship. Instead, this woman is identified by a physical infirmity. The "issue of blood" was her most predominant and consuming reality: it defined her personhood and controlled her existence.

The other fact that we know about this woman is that the "flow of blood" had been active for twelve years. As a result, this woman had been deprived of an essential life-giving fluid for more than a decade. It is likely that her energy level was low and that she suffered from other physical symptoms, such as anemia, fatigue, weakness, infections, dizziness, and headaches. She even faced the threat of death as a result of her continued loss of blood.

Perhaps even more devastating than her physical condition were the social and spiritual consequences that were operative in the life of this woman. The laws of that day dictated that menstrual bleeding made a woman ritually unclean (Leviticus 15:19-30) as well as everything she touched. In addition to being ill, this woman was condemned to live in seclusion much like the lepers of that day. Even if she had once been married and had children, she could no longer be a part of their lives. She was not even permitted to enter the temple for worship. Imagine being cut off from your family, your friends, and your church. Her condition had cut her off from all humanity and divinity.

Another ramification of her illness was poverty. She may have been wealthy at one time (Mark 5:26; Luke 8:43), but all of her money and earthly possessions may have been used up seeking medical care for her condition. Yet none of the physicians had been able to provide a cure for her. Instead, the bleeding continued and her condition grew worse.

This woman's physical condition, resulting isolation, and poverty had surely resulted in a degree of emotional damage. Most anyone who is despised, rejected, and made to feel inferior and unclean begins to suffer emotionally. It can be easily surmised that by-products of this woman's suffering may have included low self-esteem, self-pity, self-hatred, anger, anxiety, depression, and hostility. She could not love herself because she had not received love for a long time. She may have spent many days and nights crying and cursing the day she was born. Keeping any semblance of sanity must have been a daily challenge.

Despite her isolation from society, this woman managed to get the word that Jesus was passing through town. Disillusioned with doctors, her desperation moved her to seek healing through her own initiative. In response to the report that Jesus was a man of miracles, she attempted to get to him. Her instinct told her that if she could just get to Jesus and touch the hem of his garment, she would be healed. Prior to her encountering him, she had the faith to believe that mere contact with his clothes would be sufficient. Her plan was an audacious and risky one, because she would violate social codes for proper female behavior and would break religious law. Anything she touched, including Jesus, was believed to be tainted by her impurity; moreover, a woman touching a man, especially in public, was unheard of. Nevertheless, this woman took the risk, ascended from her home of isolation, and walked through the streets. When she found Jesus, this physically weak woman mustered the strength to reach out and touch the hem of his robe.

Scripture tells us that the very moment the woman touched Jesus' clothes, her flow of blood ceased and she knew that her healing had come (Mark 5:30; Luke 8:44). Jesus immediately discerned that his body had also changed and that "power" had just gone from his body. He asked, "Who touched me?" This question seemed almost foolish in the midst of such a large crowd, and the disciples said as much (Mark 5:31; Luke 8:45). The disciples' impatience bespoke their desire to be about the business at hand, which was accommodating the male, Jarius, whose daughter had been brought to Jesus for healing. Jesus refused to disregard the touch and called the woman forth to make her healing public. Jesus wanted to see her full restoration to the religious and social community. He insisted that she reveal her identity.

The woman came forward in obedience and fell at Jesus' feet, confessing her deed and acknowledging her healing (Mark 5:33; Luke 8:47). The bold and aggressive behavior she displayed earlier was replaced with fear and trembling. Immediately, Jesus affirmed this woman by calling her "daughter." This affectionate term was used to reassure her that she was now a part of Israel. He then informed her that her faith in God had provided her healing and that she could now know peace and wholeness (Mark 5:34).

A womanist reading of this text sees in this woman every African American woman who has been marginalized because of her race, gender, poverty, and other social conditions. From the beginning of our lives here in this country, our black skin has relegated us to a life much like the one this woman must have led. African American women have been made to feel dirty, inferior, and unworthy to participate fully in society. Slavery, Jim Crow and Jane Crow laws, lynchings, unprovoked beatings, and mysterious murders have been our experience. Segregated water fountains, restroom facilities, and lunch counters have been the symbols of our "uncleanness." Our exclusion from the mainstream of humanity has robbed us of opportunities of economic development, adequate education, and decent living conditions. Loss of pride, self-esteem, self-respect, and culture has resulted in an inauthentic and oppressed existence.

Women and men of the black church have strongly identified with this woman because we are people "with an issue of blood." Indeed, the black church as a whole has so pervasively acknowledged this woman's suffering and healing because she is one who speaks directly to our condition and experience. She is one whose life we live and whose sorrow we feel. Her suffering is best felt by a people who suffer. Her desperation and frustration are the embodiment of African American people's intense desire for wholeness and restoration to legitimate personhood. Her healing and affirmation by Jesus sustain the hope that the African American community has for continued divine intervention and approval. She is the prototype of faith, humility, tenacity, and determination that we who are engaged in the human struggle are challenged to emulate and imitate.

Because this woman's faith and determination effected her healing, she is the one who shows us how to turn our tragedies into triumph and sorrow into joy. The desperate act of defying religious and social tradition, of risking her life to gain a better one, and emptying herself of shame and fear empowers us to appropriate her desperation and courage and press toward wholeness. To see this woman as merely a victim is to misunderstand the courage and tenacity it took for her to defy social mores and, in spite of her own despair, take a bold move toward Jesus.

PART 2

Sermons for Healing

5

It's Time to Leave Absalom's House

2 Samuel 13:1-20

"As for me, where could I carry my shame?"
—2 Samuel 13:13

Shame is a debilitating and damaging emotion that plagues humanity. It is a state of mind that steals many women's joy. Feelings of embarrassment, degradation, and humiliation have been consuming and ever-present forces in the lives of little girls, teens, and adult women around the world. Shame has been a toxic reality that has crushed our souls and forced us into a mental and emotional prison, keeping us separated from ourselves, our loved ones, and our God. Many women have never known authentic abundance or spiritual prosperity because they have been tied up, tangled up, and boxed in by unhealthy and life-taking shame.

So many sisters—sisters who have the appearance of success and contentment—have not known inner peace or joy for a long time because some act or some circumstance over which they had no control has forced them to live in shame. *He* raped you; *she* molested you. Yet you somehow feel as though you are to blame. You are the one going through life feeling so devalued, damaged, or diminished that you cannot climb out of a place of spiritual and emotional isolation. You are the one who doesn't have the confidence to assume your rightful place in God's realm.

You were the injured party, the innocent one, the victim of circumstance, but for years you have been carrying the weight of someone else's sin. For years, dealing with these feelings has made it extremely difficult for you to find and fulfill your purpose. You haven't been able to tell anyone. You have been carrying this *thing* everywhere you go. Hardly a day passes that the memory of the trauma or the reality of ongoing abuses does not arise, haunting you.

Webster's Dictionary defines *shame* as "the painful feeling arising from the consciousness of something dishonorable, improper, or disgraceful done by oneself or another." It is self-condemnation or self-devaluation. It is putting oneself down and becoming consumed by extreme feelings of inadequacy and inferiority. It is a spoken or unspoken declaration that there is something in me that makes me unacceptable; there is something about my life that makes me less valuable. I am irrationally engulfed in a deluge of mental anguish. I have heart wounds that keep me in a perpetual state of mourning, dreading the day that the source of my shame will be exposed. Those who know shame often want to disappear from the face of the earth. Most times, the heavy burden of shame is carried in isolation.

In the spirit of Christian truth and compassion, it is the assignment of the church and the prophet to place liability appropriately where liability belongs. God would have those who have known the heartache of sexual abuse, domestic violence, or family chaos come to an understanding that the culpability is not with those who have been raped, battered, or abandoned. Rather, the culpability is with the one who did the raping, battering, or abandoning. However, the prophet must also convey to the wounded that being taken advantage of and wounded by another cannot dominate one's emotional and spiritual disposition to the point that those acts are responsible for permanent loss of self-confidence, self-love, or God-given sexual identity. All of us are still fearfully and wonderfully made, in spite of our devastating experiences. We must not allow our pain to tell us otherwise. God has still put God's Spirit in us, and we cannot miss the biblical truth that declares that our past and present realities are never meant to abort our purpose in God. Indeed, God's plan is to give us a hope and a future (Jeremiah 29:11).

The divine revelation for every sister, wife, and daughter who has been controlled by feelings of shame is that it is God's desire for all of God's daughters to experience joy and healthy self-esteem. You are not inextricably tied to the past. Today you can begin to walk in godly abundance. You can decide that bitterness, embarrassment, and regret will not squeeze the life out of you. You do not have to continue to live with shame.

It is important to point out that some shame can be productive and corrective, motivating us to healthier living. When a person's private choices or mistakes come to light, shame can drive him or her to be more self-disciplined or to behave more appropriately. However, perpetual feelings of shame have rendered too many of us emotionally arrested and spiritually dysfunctional. This type of shame must be eliminated—for women who have been victims of another's sin but carry the burden of that transgression, women who are living in abusive situations, men who were abandoned by a parent, children who were born into toxic realities, or mothers whose children made the wrong choices. When shame invades the soul, depletes the spirit, and distorts the personality, it becomes a stronghold that makes you feel responsible for something that was not your fault and that you cannot change.

Myriad women in the church involved in ministry, anointed and established in positions of leadership, are wounded by shame for a variety of reasons. Their husbands cheat, but they believe that the man's adultery is an indictment against them. Shame causes them to withdraw from God and the church. Some women listen to society's definition of beauty, and when their body size, body shape, hair texture, and skin color do not meet defined requirements, shame gives birth to self-hatred. When a son goes to jail or a daughter becomes pregnant by a married usher, their mothers feel responsible, and those feelings rob them of inner peace or fulfillment. Shame wounds make women weak and self-pitying. These women often tend to overcompensate and settle for less than they deserve. Shame wounds have caused young girls to marry wrong, become self-mutilators, and grow to be sexually promiscuous. Others have suffered bulimia, anorexia, or obesity as a result of being unable to love themselves properly.

The blessing for those who are determined to walk in God's abundance is in beginning to understand that no matter what wounds we have sustained in our lives from shame and guilt, no matter how long we have contended with feelings of inferiority, self-blame, or embarrassment, God is calling us to a higher level of living. We must embrace the truth that we have the power to forsake our tendencies to beat ourselves up about that which is past and all those things over which we have no control. We must come to the place where we walk in the knowledge that we will be at our best as women, as sisters, as wives, as mothers, and as servants of the Lord when we overcome shame and guilt and other negative feelings about ourselves. Our aim as women must be to seek God and see ourselves as God wants us to be.

The story of Tamar provides an example of a woman consumed with shame. She experienced one of the greatest violations a woman can ever sustain. Hers is a story of lust, selfishness, and immoral sensual gratification. Disgrace, dishonor, and rejection were her plight. Family dysfunction, male abuse, and female suffering were her reality. Her life was one of mental anguish, emotional wounding, and paralyzing shame that came with parental detachment, fraternal rape, and lack of family support. The story of Tamar speaks to every woman who has ever been objectified or devalued; every woman who has taken on the burden of having to suffer quietly for another's actions; every woman who has had to withdraw, had to be silent, had to struggle to live beyond her shame, guilt, and depression. One way or another, this woman speaks to all of us who have ever been violated, hurt, or abused.

The facts are these: Amnon, Absalom, and Tamar were three of David's children. History records that Absalom and Tamar's mother was Princess Maacah, and Amnon's mother was Ahinoam. Tamar was an extremely lovely young woman. As she grew more beautiful, her half brother Amnon developed a driving sexual passion for her. So strong was his desire for her that the Scripture records that he began to grow sick and obsessed. Eastern tradition dictated that virgins were to be kept in seclusion. Thus, it was supposedly impossible for Amnon to touch Tamar. That likely made him want her all the more.

Amnon's cousin Jonadab observed that Amnon had begun to look haggard and thin. When he inquired about this look of distress, Amnon told Jonadab of his desire for Tamar. Jonadab, whom the Bible describes as a crafty man, was as debased as Amnon. Jonadab devised a plan by which Amnon could rape Tamar. So brother and cousin plotted to violate Tamar. Human cruelty conceived in the womb of family is always more wounding and heinous, for it is seeded by familiarity and availability.

Jonadab instructed Amnon to pretend to be ill and to ask his father, David, for permission for Tamar to prepare food for him. As inappropriate as this request was, David accommodated his son. And when Amnon got Tamar alone, he grabbed her and began to overpower her.

She begged, "Please do not do this thing to me. Such a thing should not be done in Israel." This is no doubt a reference to Leviticus 20:17, which says that if a man marries or has sexual relations with his sister, it is a disgrace and they must be cut off before the eyes of the people. Tamar desperately tried to reason with Amnon. "Don't do this wicked thing. Think of what it will cost me. What about me? How can I live beyond this disgrace? And you! You will lose your right to the throne." She pleaded and reasoned to no avail. Lust and a sense of male entitlement dismissed her pleas, and Amnon raped his sister.

Amnon's lust overruled sound moral judgment. After it was over, the Bible says that Amnon hated Tamar intensely. He had gotten what he wanted. After taking her dignity and stealing her dreams, he rejected her in the worst way. All of the love that he previously professed for her dissipated. He had wanted her when she was untouched. Yet after defiling her, Amnon cast Tamar aside (perhaps already in search of another woman to wound).

Sending her away would give the public the impression that it was Tamar who was the evil one. It would suggest that she had played the harlot and seduced him. By being sent away, Tamar was doubly violated. Not only had she been raped, but she would be implicated as the seductress, forced to bear her shame alone.

Aware of what being sent away would mean for her, Tamar protested further, saying, "To send me away would be a greater wrong than what you have already done to me." Tamar must have thought, "If you send me away, you are treating me like the criminal, and it will be assumed that I am the evil one." But Amnon would not listen.

To cover up his own sin, Amnon commanded one of his male servants to remove Tamar from the house. "Get this woman out of here, and bolt the door behind her." And so the servant sent her away. Utterly distraught, Tamar put ashes on her head as a sign of mourning and tore her royal garments as a sign that her position of royalty had not saved her or perhaps as a sign that she was no longer a virgin. Tamar went on her way, weeping aloud.

Eventually, she met up with her brother, Absalom. Her countenance was such that he recognized immediately what had occurred, and he asked if she had been with Amnon. Tamar dropped her head in shame, confirming the violence that she had sustained at the hand of their brother. Yet instead of showing compassion and consolation, Absalom challenged her to do two very irrational and emotionally violent things.

First, he told her, "Keep quiet! For this is your brother." Then he added, "Do not take this thing to heart." Not only did Absalom tell Tamar to keep silent about her pain, but he even went so far as trivializing the sexual violence that had been perpetrated against her by her own brother. Absalom's response is not unlike the response that women who live with shame have experienced.[1]

Throughout the ages, women have been forced into conspiracies of silence. We have been unfairly burdened with the charge to keep peace in the family and save those who wound us from disgrace and scandal. All too often those who have been sinned against are mandated not to make a fuss or call attention to an act of human defilement. In some families even today, the need to avoid scandal is greater than the desire for justice and honesty. The conspiracy of silence gives women a message that their victimization is unworthy of attention, their plight is unimportant; they need to "suck it up" and "get over it."

Like many who are forced to suffer in silence, the Bible says that Tamar went off to Absalom's house a desolate woman. Suffering in silence can force the strongest woman (even a woman like Tamar, whose name means "palm tree," a symbol of strength, adaptability, and the ability to thrive in dry places) into a desolate place. There are some things in this life that drain us of every bit of resilience; there are some hurts from which we do not easily recover. So, like many who are forced to suffer in silence, a dejected and despondent Tamar withdrew from the rest of the world and remained at Absalom's house, a desolate woman.

Scripture does not tell us whether Tamar pined away and grew old, never able to comprehend her value or inner strength. But like anyone who has been put to shame, her heart must have been broken, her trust in God tattered. Shame locked her behind closed doors never to be seen again.

I wish that Tamar were here today so that I could give her a word about how to leave Absalom's house behind her. Women all over the world are living in Absalom's house. We have spent years in the place of our hurting, sorrow, self-flagellation, and perpetual guilt. But God's word to those who are in the quagmire of self-pity and shame-based behavior is that you are not a hopeless failure. Today is the day you must decide to have power over compulsions, addictions, and codependencies that have prevented you from moving toward your best self. We may bear Tamar's shame, but we can come out of Absalom's house. We do not have to keep silent about the experiences that make us ashamed. Once our silence is broken, we can begin to live free of the shame that enslaves us. Absalom's house does not have to become our way of life. We can escape it or even avoid it altogether.

God has the power to deliver us through God's inexhaustible resources. God can touch, heal, and be the "lifter of our heads." Gilead was the place that produced a balm known for its healing properties. Likewise, it was the place to which people fled when they were in trouble. It was a place of refuge for Jacob when he fled from Laban; it is the place where David fled when being pursued by his enemies. God is also calling us today to move from a desolate place of Absalom's house to the healing place of Gilead. We are too valuable to forever contemplate our disgrace; we are too significant to be enslaved by negative thoughts and self-perception. God is our refuge and strength, a present help in the time of trouble. As we embrace our "daughtership" as children of God, we can forever be released from the shame that binds us. It's time to leave Absalom's house behind us!

Note
1. The Bible does relate another response of Absalom to Amnon's violation of Tamar. Second Samuel 13:23 notes that *two full years* later, Absalom plotted the murder of Amnon—allegedly to avenge his desolate sister but effectively moving Absalom himself one step nearer to the throne.

6

The Power of "Enough"

Genesis 29:31-35

She conceived again and bore a son, and said, "This time I will praise the LORD."
—Genesis 29:35

nough, starring Jennifer Lopez, is one of my favorite movies. In it Lopez plays a character named Slim who is married to an unfaithful and abusive man. Their relationship begins wonderfully with a storybook courtship, wedding, and honeymoon. But the honeymoon soon ends with the husband's adultery and selfish behavior. After the birth of their daughter, Slim is forced to contend with the angry blows and cruel behavior of her mentally disturbed but wealthy husband. It is a nightmare.

He beats her, then says that he loves her. He cheats on her but makes her feel that his cheating, like his beatings, is what she deserves. As is typical, his abuse is followed by repentance and declarations of love. The cycle continues with each beating more brutal than the preceding one. When Slim tries to break free, her husband prevents her departure, only to inflict more perverted displays of temper and contempt. She is a prisoner in her marriage and her home.

Not only is this woman abused physically, but she is also abused verbally. Emotionally and mentally manipulated, she is constantly told: "It's your fault. You deserve it. You make me have to hit you." And of course, her husband uses the famous line "I will kill you if you try to get away from me." Slim becomes a woman who is sadly frightened, timid, and living in the emotional prison of low self-esteem.

She eventually attempts to get away with her daughter; however, when she changes her identity, either he or one of his violent friends finds her, and she has to flee again. She remains his prisoner.

One day, in the midst of her depression and despair, Slim has a change of attitude. Everything that has happened *to* her finally causes something to happen *within* her. As a result, her life begins to change. She is afraid and feels absolutely helpless, and she would have resigned herself to the seeming ubiquitous influence and power of her husband for the rest of her life. But one day she experiences the inner power that comes with saying, "Enough!" For it is when Slim makes up her mind that she has had enough that everything in her life begins to fall into place.

It is when she decides that she has run enough, hidden enough, cried enough, and lost enough that her life takes on new direction. It is when she understands that she has begged enough, apologized enough, kept quiet enough, and blamed herself enough that she finds the strength to take charge of her circumstances. When she finally understands that she has to find a way to take charge of her life and all of its madness in order to live the life she wants to live, and when she has a change of self-perception, she is able to move from a place of victimization to victory.

What happens to make the difference? Well, it seems that one day something jolts Slim's spirit, pushing her toward the woman she had never had the nerve to become. She starts to have confidence in herself. Her desire for deliverance and self-improvement motivate her to move to a better place. Life and its abuses have trampled her self-esteem, self-love, and hope for personal growth. One day she has an "ah-ha" moment.

Something inside Slim makes her realize that if she does not overcome some inner weaknesses, she will never move out of her place of oppression. She is clear that her husband is not going to give up or change, so the only way she is going to be free requires her to change. She develops a plan. She gets some financial assistance from her long-lost father, sends her little girl away with a friend, and enrolls in a self-defense class. She trains for many weeks. Her teacher and mentor instructs her how to kick, punch, and duck. She develops courage and speed. With each day her confidence increases, her self-esteem is raised, and her determination is intensified.

She finally reaches the point where she is ready to work her plan. She travels back to the city where they had lived and breaks into his home, and while he is away at work, she sets the stage for her attack. She removes all of the guns in his arsenal. She familiarizes herself with the layout of his apartment and waits for his return. And when he gets home, she wages a deliberate and systematic attack on him. To his amazement and indignation, she who had always backed down is backing down no more. They fight back and forth. When an opportunity presents itself for him to kill her, he tries to bludgeon her to death. Then it hits her: it is either crush or be crushed. She gets a surge of power, jumps up, and shoves him with all of her might. He crashes into the rail, breaking it and falling to his death. She is finally free of her tormentor. It is an accident that sets her free.

To be clear, I am *not* celebrating the death of the abuser; however, I do celebrate this woman's realization that she has to take charge of her messy and miserable life and find a better way to live. I celebrate the fact that when she decides that she has lived with violence, weakness, and unhappiness long enough, she reaches down into her untapped inner resources and finds a power that has been hidden from her by her circumstances. As a result, she lifts herself out of a mental and emotional rut and frees herself of long-standing bondage. We must remember that we are not so weak or oppressed by sin and sorrow that we cannot turn our situation around.

The word of the Lord to every woman who has spent too much time settling for relationships, jobs, and situations that are not fulfilling, nurturing, or true to your potential is that there is power in deciding you have had enough. Today is the day for women to realize that we can create a better life for ourselves by clearing our space of emotional clutter and the people who create a toxic internal reality. How much better our lives will be when we stop subjecting ourselves to environments and personalities that take away our freedom and self-esteem.

God is calling for brave and determined women to adopt an attitude of intolerance for those things in their lives that abuse, confuse, and restrict. Our divine Provider is just waiting for some of us to say, "I am not going to go on like this. I am ready to walk in my privilege and break though to a new way of being." God is just waiting to work in us and with us to replace fear with self-confidence, guilt and shame with the determination to be better, and low expectation for self to a conviction that says, "I am better than this, so I can do better than this."

Let's examine the text. Genesis 29 tells the story of a homely and mistreated woman named Leah. Leah was Jacob's first wife and Rachel's sister. From the very beginning, Jacob did not love Leah; he loved her younger sister, Rachel. But Laban, Leah and Rachel's father, felt that his older daughter should get married first, so he tricked Jacob into marrying Leah. While Jacob was married to Leah, it was Rachel who had his heart. Jacob pursued Rachel until she was his wife, too. Rachel was his woman of choice, while Leah was a woman of convenience, for although he did not love her, he did sleep with her.

The writer of this biblical story implies that Leah spent a lot of her mental and emotional energy trying to find love in this love-impoverished situation. Rejection is never easy to take. It is especially devastating in your own home or spiritual community. Leah did everything she could to live up to Jacob's standards so that she could find a place in his heart. Since Leah was not very pretty, I imagine she spent a lot of time trying to make herself attractive to Jacob. In her mind, Rachel was the competition. Yet in reality, she would never be able to compete with the beautiful sister for Jacob's love.

Day after day, Leah concentrated on Jacob, Rachel, and her personal misery. The Bible says that when God saw that Leah was not loved, God opened her womb. Perhaps the blessing of reproduction was designed to make her see that sometimes you have to create new life for yourself apart from the one that cannot give you what you need.

When Leah gave birth to her first son, her thoughts were only of Jacob and her misery. She named him Reuben, which means "surely my husband will love me now." Her son's name is an indication of her desperation. She had another son, but his birth gave Leah no joy or self-appreciation. All she could see in the midst of divine creation was "because the Lord saw that I am hated, God gave me Simeon." She had a third son, but still she was controlled by fear, poor judgment, and emotional dysfunction, and she was never able to celebrate the creative process that was God's gift to her to motivate her to emotionally connect to herself. Instead, her response to God's blessing upon the birth of Levi was "Now my husband will become attached to me because I have given him three sons."

Somewhere between the third and the fourth pregnancy, it appears that Leah experienced a spiritually motivated personal transformation. One day a defining moment gave birth to a change of attitude. This change of attitude changed her focus and reshaped her inner reality. For the first time, she was able to get in touch with who she really was. She realized that her life had to be bigger than Jacob. She had enough of trying to deny who she was and trying to be who Jacob wanted her to be.

The text reveals that by the time Leah gave birth to her fourth son, her thoughts were not about Jacob first. She had finally had enough of feeling sorry for herself, enough of being depressed because she was not desirable to a man who never loved her to begin with, enough of feeling guilty and ashamed. This time she was in touch with reality. This time she was clear that she could not make Jacob love her, but she could make Leah love Leah. The new Leah vowed with the birth of Judah, "This time I will praise the LORD."

Can you hear Leah declaring, "I cannot grow as long as I am obsessing over how another person feels about me. I cannot find my best self as long as I see myself through Jacob's eyes. I cannot find God until I clear the clutter out of my life. I have realized that my life is bigger than Jacob. *This* time I will praise the Lord."

So many women have some "Jacobs" in their lives that they need to put in proper perspective. Jacob is that person, experience, or memory that prevents you from appreciating the woman that you are and discovering the purpose that is yours. Like Leah, you need to decide that your life is bigger than that one sexual encounter, that experience of date rape, or that job promotion you didn't get. You are not defined by another person's opinion of you, your divorce, or your husband's numerous seasons of infidelity. Your relationship with God will empower you to see who you really are.

With this change of attitude, in addition to giving birth to Judah, Leah gave birth to the new Leah. When she found the courage to declare "Enough!" and when she saw the self-destructive nature of her thinking and decided to change her attitude, she was empowered to find her best self and worship the Lord. She walked away from a desperate, insecure, and needy Leah and found the Lord, and when she found the Lord, she found a new Leah.

Every woman who is ready to walk away from situations that are abusive and dead, who is ready to dream big, think judiciously, and live out of the box, and who is committed to not apologizing for her gifts must understand her responsibility to realistically and spiritually access her life and see how much better it can be when she identifies the sources of her bondage and decides that "enough is enough." For every Leah who is ready to be free of bad habits, negative attitudes, and ungodly behaviors that keep her in bondage, things can change when she draws the line and begins to walk in godly strength.

You have lived underneath the weight of oppression and suppression long enough, and you will experience life anew when you begin to stand up for yourself and stand up in God. Become a real fighter and force with which to contend in this spiritual war for your life. If you want to grow and get out of life's ruts, you must battle daily with negative thoughts about yourself and forgive yourself for past mistakes. Know that God is going to give you the strength that you need to get the job done. God is committed to your growth, liberation, and moral well-being.

To be weak, self-debasing, and insecure is to be carnally minded. To let men lie to you and women deceive you is to be carnally minded. To say that I cannot go to school, I cannot leave him, and I am not able to improve is to be carnally minded—and a carnal mind is enmity against God. When you are truly seeking God, you cannot settle for anything that is inferior or substandard. When your mind is being transformed, you will be renewed and will no longer be imprisoned by your attitude and thoughts. You will begin to tell yourself you have worried enough, agonized enough, taken enough, justified enough, and begged enough.

Although you may have dealt with a lot and been through a lot, you are stronger than everybody says you are. You will only live life at its best when you decide that you are at a place of enough. It is only when we learn and accept the truth about ourselves and the circumstances that surround us that we make progress. It is only when we get fed up with the unproductive, abusive, negative, and oppressive behaviors that lead to failure that we can forge ahead. We can break away from the stuff that ushers us into dangerous territory so that we can thrive and find help for a brighter future. Sometimes we cannot wait for deliverance; we have to fight for it. We have to break free of some relationships, some friendships, some guilt, and some shame to get to the next level. Being women of God requires that we recognize our own oppression and our own destructive and ungodly behavior. When you are really walking with the Lord, you will eventually get to the place that you know that your survival and growth depend on your ability to say, "No more!"

To the Leahs and Slims who are fed up with being abused by life and determined to find a more excellent way, this is the time for something wonderful to happen. Make a vow to God today, declaring, "I am giving myself over to an internal makeover, and it is my change on the inside that is going to help me work on some stuff that is going down on the outside. I am appropriating the God-essence that is in me so that I might defeat oppressive forces that seek to mess up my life." Reject the spirits of apathy, failure, and lies that have hidden God's truth in your life. Denounce the spirits of fear and defeat. Know that God has enough love, joy, peace, and unmerited favor to turn your life around. And this time, release God's power within. And like Leah, this time praise the Lord. God is enough. You are enough. Enough is enough!

7

I Have to Keep Moving

Genesis 19:1-8, 15-17, 24-26

But Lot's wife...looked back.
—Genesis 19:26

Relationships can bring out either the best or the worst in people. Marriage, friendship, or other associations can either show us our optimal selves or cause us to become defensive, angry, overly suspicious, or stressed out. In healthy relationships, we can grow and discover new ways of being; we can learn to overcome weaknesses and conquer self-centered living. On the other hand, in dysfunctional relationships, we can find ourselves becoming more apathetic, cynical, anxious, jaded, bitter, or spiteful than we ever imagined. Relationships often shape our personalities, establish our expectations, or determine where we stand spiritually and emotionally. A good relationship has the potential to open us to abundant living. On the other hand, an unhealthy relationship can cause ulcers and nervous breakdowns or make us feel that the only way to deal with the relationship is to buy a ticket to nowhere.

I have often said that for me marriage, motherhood, and friendship have been the mirrors that have shown me who I am and who I need to become. It is through relationships that I realized my tendencies to be selfish, inflexible, and overly sensitive—traits that stem from my being an only child. It is in marriage that I realized I was a good talker but not always a good listener. I came to understand that I needed to work on my conversational tone and that there were some opinions I just needed to keep to myself. After I was married for a while, I realized that if we were going to make it, I would have to learn the art of compromise, effective problem solving, and adapting to unexpected change. Some of the things that I said I could never do, I have had to do for the sake of the relationship. Because of the lessons I have learned in relationships, I am not the person I was thirty years ago.

God puts us in relationships so that we can grow and keep moving toward our best selves. Having loved and been loved, we should be more sensitive, generous, and trustworthy today than we were yesterday. Many of us can testify that a loving husband or a college roommate has given help that we needed to move beyond bad experiences, troubled beginnings, or parental mistakes. Having a spouse, a friend, or even a good parent has made many of us more confident, more creative, and more aware of our strengths and weaknesses.

On the other hand, others of us would have to confess that we used to be nice and easygoing until we met "that person." It could be a boss, a coworker, or even a spouse; but having to deal with that person has made us stubborn, spiteful, and secretive. Perhaps you used to be nice until verbal abuse or constant put-downs made you moody and sharp-tongued. Deep down you are a loving person, but mental and verbal abuse have made you defensive, and now you are making someone else pay for the abuse you suffered at the hands of another. The relationship is so depleting and wounding that you have become the very person you said you would never become. You never used to be sarcastic. You did not enter your marriage with low-self esteem. The pain and disappointment of marriage, parenting, or other relationships have caused you to do things, say things, and think things you never used to do, say, or think. There are many women, even Christian women, who have become stagnant and stationary because someone has had such a negative impact on us that we are unable to reach our potential.

Indeed, many of us admittedly have allowed a husband, mother-in-law, child, or significant other to bring out the worst in us. Our feelings about another person have boxed us into a space of anger, shame, or insecurity from which we cannot move.

In spite of what we have become because of our relationship, the word of the Lord to all is that it is essential and possible for women to access the power of God in our lives. Although life will challenge the human spirit, focused and determined women must persistently seek to move toward healthy change. We must move away from self-imposed limitations to a greater dependence on God. God will empower us to become the strong and productive women God intended us to be.

When women are open to the move of God, wounds will be healed and unhealthy emotions will be restored. Weaknesses can be repaired and broken hearts can be mended. We can begin to see ourselves as God sees us and discover the women God wants us to be. God never intended for women to let life overpower them; we were created to perform wondrous works that will make us a blessing to all with whom we come in contact. For the sake of our marriages, our children, our loved ones, and the community of the faithful, we believers must change the way we think about others and ourselves. We must mentally and spiritually move away from the troubles and disappointments of our past.

Life is filled with constant change, and if change has alienated you from the person God made you, I want to remind you that you must not lose your sense of self to someone who does not contribute to your higher level of living. When a loved one puts you down, you must rise above it. When a friend or child disappoints you or a boyfriend walks away from you, there is still room in your emotional space for your power to shine through. When things go wrong, stay right, walk down God's path to deliverance, and let God build you up in all your crushed and overwhelmed places. Throughout the church, there are women who have feelings that have stymied and halted their progress. They may be shouting and singing, giving the impression that they are growing in God, when in fact far too many are stuck—stuck because of the secrets with which they have been living or because someone doesn't satisfy their needs or because they cannot forgive.

Because every woman is too important for God to lose to negative feelings and behavior, God is on a mission to breathe health into unhealthy self-perceptions, to make good marriages better, to heal hurts and give every disillusioned person a new sense of purpose. There is too much at stake for women of purpose to allow another's actions to push them to perpetual states of anger, resentment, or low self-esteem. We are in a fight for our souls and minds, and the key to successful and abundant living is to know that it is not profitable for us to cling to past hurts. We have every reason to move forward. We can't let the one who left us, betrayed us, or wounded our spirit keep us in an ungodly place. There will be times in our lives when we will just have to tell ourselves, in spite of everything, "I am going to keep on moving."

The story of Lot's wife shows us just how important it is to keep moving. Lot's wife is a woman whom history records as disobedient and sin-loving. Her "glance back" toward Sodom is seen by preachers and scholars alike as an attachment to sin. While that may be an accurate portrayal, recently as I reread this text, it occurred to me that something else may have been driving this woman. Let us look at the story.

The Bible records that Lot was at the city gate when two men (angels, messengers) appeared. Lot invited the men to his home. Soon after their arrival, some other men from the city came to the house demanding that Lot give his guests over to them for sexual intercourse. Household codes of that day required that a host make his home safe for his guests. So Lot, appalled and determined to protect his guests from these sexual predators, impetuously offered his two virgin daughters over to them to satisfy their lust. This was a violent and wounding gesture on Lot's part. The humiliation those young girls must have experienced when their father offered their bodies to these men cannot be denied.

While the Bible does not mention Lot's wife during this episode, I would have to think that even if she was not there, she heard about this incident. As a mother of two daughters myself, I would also imagine that the knowledge of Lot's reckless and irresponsible behavior enraged and disgusted his wife. He offered her daughters to satisfy the pleasure of a group of perverted strangers. I wonder how she felt about him and their marriage in light of this situation. Was this the man she married? Was this the father of her children? Even from the beginning of time, it was expected that parents would protect and cherish their offspring. And while sons were more valued than daughters, surely this act went against the way in which parents ought to behave toward any child, male or female. Lot's exploitation of their children undoubtedly could have angered Mrs. Lot to the point of emotionally separating from him.

My reading of this text and my experience as a wife and mother make me wonder if Lot's behavior shaped Mrs. Lot's feelings about Lot, about their future, and about their marriage. I wonder if, like some other women who have found themselves being emotionally neglected, disappointed with, or betrayed by a loved one or otherwise trapped in an unbalanced relationship, Mrs. Lot decided to throw in the emotional towel. I wonder if she simply gave up and decided to stop moving.

If we examine the rest of the story, we discover such may have been the case. When the divine mandate came for the destruction of Sodom and Gomorrah, giving Mrs. Lot and her family the opportunity to flee destruction, it is possible that she found herself at a place of ambivalence and detachment. Do I go with this person who has hurt and disappointed me, or do I stay? Do I move into the future and realize new possibilities, or do I stand still in my anger and frustration?

I am certain that many of us who have come to similar crossroads in our lives can relate to Mrs. Lot's frustration and trepidation.

Do I let that father or mother or spouse who has proven to be selfish, unwise, and irresponsible harden me and make me afraid to live? Or do I learn from that season of my life and keep on evolving and moving forward? Most of us who have ever been in a relationship where things have gone wrong may have found ourselves paralyzed with feelings that prevented our growth and improvement. We came to a crossroads where we had to decide either to participate in our own demise or keep on moving. At that crossroads, we turned to God.

The good news is that if you are twisted, the Lord will straighten you out. If you are damaged, God will rebuild your confidence. If you are in bondage, God will set you free to keep moving. Grace and mercy want to take you to a higher plain where you can truly experience the presence of God. The gift of God's love will open the door to a productive future.

Mrs. Lot had not heard the good news that we have today. And even though the angels had told Lot's family not to look back, Lot's wife did so anyway, and she became a pillar of salt. As a result, she missed out on her new beginnings. She became a prisoner to her own feelings. Something in her—maybe it was her anger at Lot, maybe it was her uncertainty about her marriage—made her stop moving. You will not like the person that you become once your stop moving. Once you get stuck in memories of the past, in the dysfunction of your relationship, you lose yourself in the process.

Lot's wife is guilty of withdrawal and avoidance. She closed everyone else out; she cut herself off from healing and new horizons. She got stuck in the past, and she lost her opportunity to discover the new truths of God. When she stopped moving, she wiped out her future.

When you stop moving, you get unexplained migraines and heart palpitations. When you stop moving, you may find yourself punishing your present husband for the sins of your child's father. When you stop moving, you may find yourself having to take blood pressure pills and valium. When you stop moving, you may start overmothering your children and trying to control your husband. Your relationships become tattered, your self-perception distorted. When you stop moving, you become fair game for the devil. You confuse lust with love, your eyes start to wander, and your priorities get distorted. But be of good courage. God's truth will heal, deliver, and move God's women to creative purpose and supernatural resurrection. God can get you moving again!

I wish the good news had been available to Lot's wife. Maybe she would have pushed through and not stopped moving. You see, when Lot's wife stopped moving, she ceased being a wife to her husband and mother to her children. Her family escaped from destruction and settled in the mountains. Though she had started the journey with them, she remained emotionally isolated—and eventually that emotional isolation became quite literal. One day her motherless daughters got their father drunk because they wanted to lay with him to preserve the family line. The perversion of their father was now seemingly driving the daughters to engage in perverted behavior. I submit that if their mother had kept on moving, she could have been there to guide her daughters and the generational curse could have been broken. Had she not given in to her feelings or had she sought help to overcome them, she could have been there to help them grow and live in God's glory.

Her children needed her, but she was unable to break free. She may not have felt she had anyone to lean on to help her rev her back up again. Her husband was not an option. He was partly her source of pain. She was in a "strange land" and had not been able to connect with some sister friends to help her move forward. Or perhaps her girlfriends had tried to help her "bounce back," but she was too far gone.

Whatever the reason, Mrs. Lot was not there for her children.

The Lord wants to use godly women to speak truth to the young and disconnected, but that can happen only when we come out of emotional isolation and keep on moving. "Mother" may be stuck, "girlfriend" may be in a rut, but with God's help we can keep on moving. We have the power to speak into our daughters' lives and tell them not to make the same mistakes we made. We can teach our sons that their mistakes can be overcome and that strongholds of addiction can be broken. Our faith in the promises of God must propel us ahead.

God offers inner peace and freedom from the deep hurts of life. God give opportunity for every woman to depart from past lies, woundedness, and every ungodly force that seeks to contaminate the purpose to which she is called. I pray that every woman in relationship will strengthen that relationship by discarding every unhealthy pattern of toxic loving. Be equal givers and equal takers. Give the love that you want to receive. Do not overlove him and underlove yourself. Do not underlove your spouse and overindulge yourself. Be true to yourself and true to the God who loves you. God will help you to move away from everything that opposes the work and the will of God. Keep moving!

8

Wounded in the House of My Friend

Zechariah 13:1-6

And if anyone asks them, "What are these wounds on your chest?" the answer will be "The wounds I received in the house of my friends."
—Zechariah 13:6

Women are constantly forced to deal with situations that "contradict their context." Home is expected to be a place of safety and conciliation. So, to experience abuse in the home at the hand of a child, parent, or sibling is a contradiction of context. Likewise, a spouse is the one who should love, respect, and protect. For a woman to experience verbal castigation, physical violence, and emotional battering from the one to whom she is married is, indeed, a contradiction of context. To be female and poor and receive inferior heath care in the hospital; to go into counseling for the healing of wounds and then experience sexual advances or financial exploitation from the counselor; or to be a neglected and demoralized senior citizen while living in the home of the child to whom one has devoted one's life is a contradiction of context. Wounds incurred in any place or under any circumstance where the expectation is that one will receive care, concern, and nurture are the hardest to bear. Such is the case when a woman is "wounded in the house of a friend."

Personal testimonies and historical accountings reveal that countless women have experienced contradictions of context in the church of the living God. In a place where there should be love, acceptance, and a celebration of all of humanity, women have experienced great levels of rejection and maltreatment. Gender oppression at the hand of priests or pastors, male leadership, and other women has been prevalent throughout Judeo-Christian history. So-called God-centered traditions have formulated patriarchal theologies that deemed menstruating women "unclean," justified the objectification of women as chattel, concubines, and matrimonial property, and made women totally dependent on men for provision and validation. It was expected that women would be silent, submissive, and sexually controlled. Even the twenty-first-century church continues to be a source of pain and a place where women are devalued and undervalued. While women have loved God and have been and continue to be committed to the work of the church, it has also been and continues to be a place where we are categorically and perpetually wounded.

Pastors' spouses, wives in particular, take more than their share of blows within the church. For years, pastors' spouses have experienced and confessed oppression from church folk. They have been forced into psychological warfare with church folk who have felt entitled to tell them what to wear, how to raise their children, and how to satisfy their men. They have had to endure the unsolicited advice of strangers, unwanted comments of those whose singular goal is to make them feel insecure and vulnerable, and often the harsh criticism of their pastor-husbands. And then there are church folk who love the pastor but despise the pastor's spouse. There are those who get angry with the pastor, and because they cannot get to him, they take it out on the wife. Yes, for many women who are married to pastors, the church has been the place of their wounding.

Women congregants and women in ministry have likewise gone to the house of God expecting it to be a place of refuge and positive interaction but instead have found it to be an environment where they are not respected or accepted as equal. Most leadership positions in many contemporary local churches are still held by men, despite the fact that women represent the overwhelming majority of those who give financially and provide service. Some church by-laws and denominational policies still forbid women to preach and pastor. Even when the ordination and appointment of women are permitted, nonegalitarian practices and sexism in the pew and pulpit have proven to women over and over again that patriarchy is alive and well in the Christian church. Even today it is primarily male pastors and church leaders who formulate theologies that convince women that their role in the church is largely to provide sex to their partners, money to the church, and unconditional loyalty to the preacher, the often-called "man of God." As a result, the church is replete with damaged and spiritually confused women. And if you were to ask these women, "What are these wounds on your soul; from whence did your scars come?" they would have to answer, "These scars were inflicted by men and women whom I loved and trusted. I was wounded in the church, in the house of my friends."

How many of us know the hurt and indignity of giving service, only to have it go unappreciated or diminished, or have been cruelly pushed aside, or have been held to a higher standard than a male counterpart? We have mentored others, only to have them leave us when things did not go their way. Those we trusted have sabotaged our work, because if they could not control it, they would rather see it destroyed.

Often women move from one contradiction of context in the church to another at home. Some women who are married to preachers are not only wounded in the church, but their pain is exacerbated at home. When husbands are abusive, unfaithful, or just a little too friendly with certain women in the church, or when they publicly celebrate their wives but privately denigrate or ignore them, the home environment becomes hellish and toxic. Because a woman's public life as a pastor's wife is somewhat addictive, she cannot leave. She becomes attached to the front pew, the public posturing, and the public recognition. She stays there. The wounds continue to mount; the scars continue to form. She smiles when she is broken on the inside, or she becomes a stiff hat-wearing "Barbie doll" who lives in denial. She cannot afford to let her guard down or to deal with the truth of her situation. Being wounded in the house of a friend is a hard thing.

Women contend with racism, social marginalization, and political dispossession. While those realities wound mind and spirit, most would concede that our deepest wounds have been inflicted by those we love.

These wounds are the most heart wrenching. The psychological battering that comes from an emotionally absent parent, insensitive grandparent, or a jealous or competitive sibling is the soul-depleting experience that really diminishes self-esteem and impedes inner peace.

How do you deal with wounds sustained in the "house of a friend"? As we address the evils and principalities that contribute to our woundedness, what can we do to heal or at least to stay sane in the meantime?

In the text as recorded in Zechariah 13, God is calling Israel to be cleansed of the sin and uncleanness that is so prevalent in the land. Yahweh is declaring that idols, false prophets, and the spirit of uncleanness would be expelled from the land. The promise is that even mothers and fathers would reject and attack their own offspring who resorted to speaking lies and prophesying without having been instructed by God to do so. The climate around ungodly prophets would be so hostile that they would do all in their power to remain anonymous. They would take off their hairy mantle and flatly deny that they were prophets. They would pretend to be tillers of the soil, and in shame they would hang their heads. And if any would see the wounds on a prophet's back that had been inflicted upon him because of his parents' wrath, he would say, "I was struck in the house of my friends." He would essentially deny who he was and seek to become someone more aligned with the Spirit of Yahweh. In this instance, the wounds speak to the prophets, reminding them of what they must do to become true followers of God.

The message inherent in the text challenges all who are on divine assignment to reject that part of themselves that is "false," change all ways that are offensive to God, and let their wounds, as undesirable as they may be, make them more determined to call on the name of the Lord.

The same is true for those who have been wounded in the church. Wounds received in the house of a friend may cause us to falter or almost give up, but they will also add prophetic depth to our lives and our purpose. They will stretch us and push us until we have learned how not to let ourselves be overcome by the trouble around us. When we develop our own relationship with God, we can overcome those things that used to keep us in turmoil. We will be less focused on what others did to wound us and more focused on the women we are becoming. Because of who God is in us, that which hurts us will also help us grow up, reach out, and calm down.

When I think about our experiences in the church, life, and personal spaces, and as I think about the pain that many of us have experienced in our familiar places, I am blessed to see that woundedness and painful situations that have arisen have not crushed our spirit but have rather given new life, built spiritual muscle, and eliminated emotional weaknesses. All around us are young women, old women, and determined women who move through the community of the faithful with authority and wisdom because they have stood up to the realities of life and ministry and decided to pursue divine potential. They have become more powerful, sturdier, and less encumbered with the weight of the wounds they have to carry. Through the power of God, we can all transcend unhealthy church cultures that would swallow us up through stereotypes and male chauvinism. What the others meant for evil can work for good, and as wounds become the womb from which ministry is birthed, the wounded open their arms to those who need our wisdom and insight.

That is why it is critical that we stay in the presence of the Lord. The Word and the love of God move us closer to human fulfillment and spiritual excellence when we give ourselves to the leading of the Holy Spirit. As we sit in worship, we must allow the Holy Spirit to confront our unhealthy emotions and our destructive behaviors. The preaching moment becomes the opportunity for us to experience the truth of God—a truth that requires us to cancel our plans for retaliation, to change our lifestyles, and to end our pity parties. No matter how broken we are, God has the power to put us back together again.

Jesus laid down his life for us, cares about us, and wants us to be stronger, wiser, and emotionally healthier. We can be healed in the house of the Lord—in the house of the greatest friend humankind has ever known.

9

Taking Possession of What's Ours
Numbers 27:1-7

They stood before Moses...and they said, "...Give to us a possession among our father's brothers."
—Numbers 27:2, 4

One of the most tragic conditions of the Christian church today is that too many members of the body of Christ have unclaimed or "unaccessed" blessings. One of the biggest travesties for some Christian women is that too many of us are living in places of lack, failure, and unfulfillment simply because we have not taken ownership of what rightfully belongs to those who are in relationship with Christ. As believers in the church today, we are exposed to a host of spiritually empowering learning experiences in our local churches and on television. Yet with all of the teaching and the "televangelizing," there is more spiritual frustration and more personal dissatisfaction among believers than ever before. People professing a thirst for God run from place to place to get the Word, but the truth is, there is seemingly more moral failure, depression, and unhappiness among women of God than there was when we did not have access to such vast spiritual resources.

When we consider the valuable riches and treasures available to us through Jesus Christ, the Word of God, and the power of the Holy Spirit, it is shameful that so many women tend to allow divine treasures and riches to escape them; so many of us allow our God-given resources to go untapped. Divine deposits have been made in all of God's daughters, deposits that were intended for kingdom purposes. However, many of our gifts and anointing have gone undetected and unused because fear, pain, and discouragement have prevented us from realizing our potential and promise.

Our Savior has gifted us with a legacy of peace, joy, love, and confidence so dynamic that all of us who know him ought to be living on top of the world. God offers us a renewed mind, a sanctified spirit, and faith-power to move mountains. Accessing those resources would put us in the place of triumphant living and spiritual wealth. The death and resurrection of Jesus provided all God's women with a legacy of power and abundance. Yet many of us have allowed trouble, cares, and concerns to shape our outlook and invade our emotional and spiritual places in ways that impede our possibility and potential. Hurts, disappointments, and shame have caused us to deny the greatness within and the opportunities without.

Indeed, many who are "called and chosen" are not doing what they could do, have not gone as far as they should have gone, have not taken possession of the territory that ought to be possessed simply because they do not understand who and whose they are. Too many don't seem to realize the truth that Paul reveals in Romans 8:17 that as children of God, we are heirs of God and joint heirs with Jesus Christ. If we are to reach our possibility and potential in this life, women of God must begin to draw from the spiritual inheritance that will empower us to live in divine protection and promise.

We read in Luke 10:19 that the Lord has given his followers power to tread on serpents and scorpions and power over the enemy. That is the promise of a spiritual strength that assures success and victory over ungodly forces that seek to destroy and deplete. But instead of treading on those forces, women have allowed forces of racism, sexism, and poverty to tread on them. Substandard education, an unjust legal system, and sexual discrimination have caused potentially strong and creative women to be oppressed, depressed, and repressed. Society-induced feelings of low self-esteem have caused well-equipped and astute women to settle for and stay in abusive relationships, bad friendships, and unfulfilling experiences in the workplace. They decrease when they should increase; they give when they should also be receiving.

God has said that those who keep their minds on God will have perfect peace, but because our thoughts are often destructive and dispiriting, numerous women who could be forgiven settle for guilt, those who could be leaders become weak-minded followers, and those who are members of a royal lineage settle for victimization and defeat. There are women all around us who live with wounds and insecurities, and those feelings have erected strongholds around their promise and expectations. Consequently, they do not have the courage or confidence to press toward the mark, seize the moment, or operate in godly authority.

It is important for every believer to remember that while there are some circumstances over which we have no control, there are others over which we have the power to exercise our godly authority and take possession of the abundant life that God intended for us to enjoy. Even though the ungodly systems of this world have been designed to make us view ourselves as inferior, unacceptable, and unworthy, it is God's will that we overcome negative stereotypes, destructive social customs, ungodly traditions, and other evil forces that keep us living beneath our potential. God's word to every woman is that we must be determined to defy every force designed to keep us from taking possession of what God wants us to have.

This message resonates in the story of the daughters of Zelophehad. These five feisty women had the audacity to take on the antifemale system and discriminatory traditions of their culture so that they could take possession of their father's inheritance. They would not hold their peace, nor would they retreat to states of impotence or inactivity.

The Bible says that Zelophehad died, leaving five daughters and no sons. While Zelophehad had acquired substantial land in his lifetime, the laws of the land stated that because he had no sons, his land would be inherited by his nearest male relative and not by his daughters. The daughters of Zelophehad decided that they would challenge the law because they believed that they were entitled to the land that had belonged to their father. It is likely that these young women had worked that land, had put their blood, sweat, and tears into it. Despite the custom of the day, they decided that justice required that they take possession of their inheritance. And so, as a united front, they went to see Moses for the purpose of laying claim to their inheritance.

They knew that women were viewed as weak and as second-class citizens and that in the eyes of many, they were voiceless and impotent.

Yet they refused to be defined or confined by the opinions of others. They would not yield to the stereotypical expectation to be well-behaved, nonthinking women. They purposed to go after that which they believed they were entitled. Perhaps they knew that well-behaved women rarely got what they deserved. So they stood before Moses and declared, "Our father died in the wilderness...and he had no sons. Why should the name of our father be taken away from his clan because he had no son? Give to us a possession among our father's brothers" (Numbers 27:3-4).

We can be sure that this kind of request was unheard of in Hebrew culture, and we would have to assert that Moses and Eleazar were taken off guard by this bold move. Nonetheless, the women stood their ground because they knew that their quality of life would be improved if they took possession of their father's land. When they stood up for themselves, things began to happen. To his credit, Moses did not give an expected misogynistic response, but instead, brought their case before the Lord. God instructed Moses, "The daughters of Zelophehad are right in what they are saying; you shall indeed let them possess an inheritance among their father's brothers and pass the inheritance of their father on to them" (Numbers 27:7).

God honored their request. These women defied a system and moved a patriarchal mountain and miraculously broke out of their place of oppression. The miraculousness of their act is further displayed when we examine the meanings of their names. The name Mahlah means "weak"; Noah means "quivering and trembling"; Hoglah means "partridge," a helpless bird; and Tirzah means "pleasant and delightful." Milcah, the only name that conveys strength or power, means "queen or ruler." From the meanings of the names of at least four of the daughters, we may assume that these were women who were timid, modest, submissive, and agreeable. They may have been when acting alone, but when those who are weak come together under the banner of a righteous cause, they can draw strength from each other. There is truly value in women walking in unity. Separate and apart the daughters may have been helpless and ineffective, but when they partnered with each other, they changed their worlds.

The resounding and timeless message to us as we strive to understand our value in a world that devalues us is clear. Through God we have the power to overcome the limitations and vulnerabilities that diminish our possibility. We owe it to ourselves to break away from relationships and lifestyles that hinder abundant living. We will rarely have it all together emotionally, intellectually, or spiritually, but our relationship with God and an understanding of our divine entitlement must motivate us to demand a better way of being.

Let us resolve together that we will not give in to any tendency to allow others to define our roles or confine our growth. Unhealthy relationships will hurt, mistakes and failures will bruise us, and cultural realities may make us forget who we are, but like the daughters of Zelophehad, we must take possession of that which is ours and partner with God, other women, and the men who esteem us to overcome systems, attitudes, and customs that steal our God-desired greatness. From this day forward, let us denounce ungodly entanglements and oppressions. Let us take possession of our healing and our inner growth. When we take possession of what is ours, God will elevate us beyond our imaginations.

10

The Diary of a Mad Black Woman

Mark 12:41-44

She...put in everything she had.
—Mark 12:44

Some time ago, Tyler Perry released a movie entitled *Diary of a Mad Black Woman*. The movie portrays the story of a woman named Helen whose husband, Charles, tells her on the eve of their eighteenth wedding anniversary that their marriage is over. Charles throws Helen out of the house and moves in his other woman, leaving his wife to fend for herself. In the weeks that follow, alone and emotionally confused, Helen is filled with anger and thoughts of retaliation.

In the midst of her anger and brokenness, however, she discovers a new woman she has never known, and in the process, she finds a new man. She struggles to overcome bitterness and to recover her dignity and her sense of purpose and place in the world. She is well on her way until the husband who rejected her is shot and left paralyzed. Out of a sense of duty, she goes to take care of him in the very house out of which she has been thrown. She proceeds to care of him until one day, looking at him sitting in his wheelchair still being nasty and sullen, the anger that she thinks she has overcome resurfaces. This "mad black woman" finds herself doing what she can to make the man who had rejected her but now needs her, suffer and crawl. She hits him, tells him off, and hits him again. She is truly a "mad black woman."

This mad black woman is a Christian who continually seeks the face of God. So even in the midst of her anger, she allows God to intercede, turning her anger into compassion. While Charles is the one who has hurt her immeasurably, she is not angry at him anymore. Instead, her experiences with him have motivated her to do something greater with her life. Instead of being passive, she becomes proactive. With the Lord's help, she makes a change and does what is good for her, something that will move her away from her painful past to embrace the promise of a new future. This mad black woman will not allow herself to feel guilty about wanting to live. Instead, she throws herself into the arms of promise and acceptance. A woman who has lived with abuse and rejection so long must sometimes force herself to expect and demand more.

There are other "mad black woman" who have not only gotten "mad" enough to change their own lives but have been mad enough to change the world. One such woman is Rosa Parks. From childhood, Rosa Parks, born in segregated Alabama, was victimized and marginalized by a racist country whose laws, customs, and disregard for social justice for African Americans pricked her very soul. Mrs. Parks was an intelligent, politically involved, and morally conscientious activist who believed that this country had to be held accountable for the way people of color were treated. She resented the fact that blacks were given literacy tests to qualify them to register to vote, while the most uneducated white man could register without being tested. She was angry when she took a literacy test for which she had diligently studied and the insipid clerk, without even looking at her answers, announced that she had failed the test. She was angry about segregated schools and public libraries that denied black students the privilege of equal education and services. She was offended that she was denied the opportunity to try on shoes before buying them and that she was required to eat at segregated lunch counters and wait in segregated waiting rooms, travel on segregated trains, and sit at the back of the bus. She was tired of seeing blacks subjected to lynchings, beatings, and unfair arrests. Yes, Rosa Parks was a "mad black woman."

Parks was not a passive, physically weary woman who would not move to the back of the bus because her feet were tired. This energetic, thoughtful, and committed activist had historically fought for human dignity and social justice. She was tired of bending to everyday racist realities, tired of being told where to drink water and where to sit, and tired of Jim Crow abuses. She was a "mad black woman." Her "madness" propelled her into action. Her declaration that she would not move ignited a movement in Montgomery, Alabama, that spread across the nation. And today, because of this "mad black woman," we enjoy many of the freedoms for which she fought and prayed.

The word *mad* often carries a negative connotation. To say that one is "mad" is to typically say that one is mentally ill, insane, frantic, or lacking in self-control and reason. But there is one definition that positively defines *mad*. To be mad is to be "angry and provoked." *Provoked* means to call forth intense feeling or to be stirred up to action. Thus, to be mad is to be internally provoked to the point of causing an external action or an altering behavior. It is to be intolerant of anything or anyone who is robbing you of your humanity; it is to resist systems and spiritual forces that seek to relegate you and yours to unacceptable and oppressive places. It is to be moved to take charge of your present space and your future place. To be mad is to be motivated to cleanse your life of anything and everything (and everybody) that seeks to make you cower and shrink. To be mad is to be determined to live. To be mad is not a focus on getting even; it is a determination to be set free. Sometimes it is good to be "mad."

If this world needs anything today, it is some mad black, Latino, and white men and women who are tired of social injustice and political hypocrisy, people who will allow their anger to provoke them to do something constructive and relevant. We need some mad black men and women who will take on spiritual wickedness in high places, who will challenge racism at the board of education and in the workplace, who will reject sexism and confront leaders who support a war in the Middle East but ignore the devastation of poor blacks in New Orleans whose lives were flooded with destructive waters. Yes, sometimes it is good to be "mad."

Chapter 12 of the Gospel of Mark tells the story of another "mad woman." She too was a woman acquainted with the pain and shame of social discrimination and community alienation. She was poor, alone, and living in a sexist and elitist society. The Bible does not give us much detail about the woman, except to say that she was a widow. In that day, the word *widow* did not merely convey the loss of a husband; it also spoke of a woman's station in life. As a widow, she was, by definition, a social outcast and a pauper. The fact that she was poor is an indication that she had no son, brother, father-in-law, or any other male relatives to support her. In that day, even if she had been married to a wealthy man, the law did not allow a woman to inherit her husband's wealth. Property was typically passed down from a man to his sons. If there were no sons, a widow often lost everything and was forced to live from hand to mouth.

The government cast her aside, the community looked down on her, and those who could have helped her, chose to knock her down. She was totally dependent on the charity of others and vulnerable to their whims. This circumstance was bound to have made feelings of rage and resentment flood her very soul. In many ways, she was the epitome of a "mad black woman" and had every right to be.

In spite of her "madness," or perhaps further evidence thereof, this woman gave everything she had to Jesus. The facts are these: Jesus sat down opposite the treasury, observing how the multitude was putting money in the treasury. The Word says that there were some rich among them who were putting in large sums of money. Then this poor widow came and placed two copper coins, amounting to one cent, into the offering box. This was all the money she had.

Taking note of what seemed to be a small act, Jesus said to the disciples, "This poor widow has put in more than all those who are contributing to the treasury. For all of them have contributed out of their abundance; but she out of her poverty has put in everything she had, all she had to live on" (Mark 12:44). Biblical scholars interpreting this text suggest that the rich gave what they had to spare, but this widow gave all that she had. She knew that "little becomes much when you place it in the Master's hand."

This woman reminds us that giving to others releases God's blessings. Some people give out of a sense of expectation. Their sole purpose for giving is to get something in return. This woman obviously gave out of love. In the process, she was giving herself a fresh start and setting the stage for new possibility.

History does not tell us what happened to this woman, but I have to believe that this act of surrender opened the door to her restoration. I have to believe that she experienced a breakthrough and turnaround in her life because she gave what she had and depended on God to give her what she needed. Her giving broke the power of the past and released the power for the future.

Let God be your everything. Let God pick up the pieces of your life. You are stronger than you think you are. You have more to give to this world than you realize. What you and the world have to gain will make up for everything you lost. God's justice and mercy will enrich your life so that like this widow you can enrich the lives of others. Be mad enough to give your all!

11

I Am Ready to Dance Again!

2 Samuel 6:12-16

*Michal daughter of Saul looked out the window, and saw
King David leaping and dancing before the LORD; and she
despised him in her heart.*
—2 Samuel 6:16

Some time ago I tuned into a movie just in time to hear a conversation between a husband and wife. In the dialogue, the husband said, "You used to dance. When we were younger, newly married, and relatively broke, you danced. You would dance around our apartment; you were light, airy, and happy. But now you never dance. What happened? Why don't you dance anymore?" he asked.

And though the wife's response to her husband was vague and evasive, I could easily deduce that the truthful answer to the question was simply this: "Life happened." Hard knocks, disappointments, hurts, and apprehension had come in with furor and stolen her dance. The lightheartedness of her youth and all of its optimism had been wiped out by compromise, problems, and losses. The flitting and exhilaration of her earlier years were crushed by the harsh realities of their life, marriage, and children. Whatever the reason, she did not dance anymore. Was it that she never thought to dance? Did she never feel like dancing? Perhaps she had so much going on in her life, so much baggage in her emotional overhead that she simply had become too constricted to dance. She, like many women, had gotten too busy, too distracted, and too encumbered to dance.

In all honesty, when I consider my own life, I have to confess that I really don't dance anymore either. I used to dance and still make noble attempts to do so, but it just is not the way it used to be. I am sure I am not the only woman in the community of faith who is guilty of losing her dance. The optimism, hope, and lightheartedness that we used to enjoy are gone. Day in and day out, we work hard, answer our critics, and deal with the mundane issues of life. We hurt, we heal, and we strive. With all we have going on, we have stopped dancing. We have had to deal with so many unanswered prayers, guard so many secrets, and do so much compromising that we no longer dance. Always second guessing the men in our lives or desperately wanting to be found by the man God told us to wait for has silenced our beat and stilled our feet. Being pulled to the left by family and to the right by profession, and feeling unnoticed and unappreciated in both arenas can weigh us down to the point that we have no desire to dance. Yes, we laugh, we tease, we sing, and we sometimes shout. But the dancing that we used to do, we don't do anymore.

It is not that we don't love God, not that we don't have the joy of the Lord, not that when the music is right and the Spirit is moving we will not break out in a dance. But truth be told, the dancing that I do now is not like the dancing I used to do "back when." I am not talking about the dances of our youth and college days, such as the Bump, the Philly Dog, or the Twist. I am talking about the dance that was born out of an excitement, enthusiasm, and zeal for life—the dance that made us unpredictable, unconventional, and untamable. It was a dance that made us defy systems, create new systems, and not worry about public opinion or peer disapproval. It was a dance that we did without music, without anyone around us, and without intending to do it. It was just a part of who we were.

I used to dance. I used to dance around my kitchen and down the street; I even used to dance with God. I had a sense of confidence, an expectation, and even a bit of fantasy-driven, faith-driven rush toward the future. When I danced, it wasn't that I did not have issues in the family or was not experiencing a certain amount of social crises. Life was not by any means perfect. Yet I had hope. I could dismiss people and be undaunted by conflict because I still believed that my current reality would eventually become a "joy in the Lord" existence. It was an "all is right with my world" twirl that would come out when I least expected. Yes, dancing wasn't merely what I did; it was who I was.

But the longer I lived, the more my world expanded, the more information I obtained, and the more I became in touch with the world's realities, the less I danced. The more I experienced racism, sexism, and cultural captivity; the more I saw a disparity in a legal system that produced prisons filled with men and women of color; the more I witnessed my sisters damaged by incest, rape, and other forms of abuse, the less I felt like dancing. The more I saw the church becoming focused on the idol of materialism than on the mandate to save souls, the more I witnessed prophets focusing on personal profit than on benefiting the poor and critiquing the systems that keep them poor, the more dancing escaped me.

The longer I lived, the more intimidated by life I felt, the more frustration I experienced, the heavier my feet got. There may have been days that I danced outwardly, but inside I really was not dancing at all. My physical dance was often an attempt to camouflage the absence of the rhythm I was feeling in my soul. Has anybody ever danced and been worried? Has anybody ever danced and been afraid? How many women have danced but been unsure of how they were going to move through their storms? Yes, many a sister has had to try to dance with the words *cancer* or *divorce* echoing in her head.

Surely, most of us can attest to the fact that the betrayal of friends, the rejection of loved ones, and "the loss of self" will make you too heavy to flit. A sick child, a mother with dementia, or an unfaithful father or husband can so burden you down that you lose your own beat. Hard work, preoccupation with church work, and dealing with personal health issues can truly take you off the dance floor, making you a proverbial wallflower. Pressure, depression, attacks, and shame will tie your hands and weigh down your spirit and your feet. Dancing will become a thing of the past.

I suppose that many of us could identify with that Mary Mary song from a few years ago that declared, "Take my shackles off my feet so I can dance," because we wished we could do just that. Shackles, or anything else that weighs us down, are not conducive to dancing. Life has taught me that at times the shackles on our feet cannot be removed by external forces, even those that are placed on us by those forces. Men, women, institutions, and systems are powerful, and they can mess with us, obstructing our lives. Yet I would have to say that the shackles that prevent us from dancing are most often the shackles that are on our minds. Shackles on our minds become shackles to our feet. Shackles on our minds will restrict our movement toward our best selves.

As I grow older, I am convinced that if I am going to please God and live the abundant life God has for me, I have to free myself to dance again. I am praying that I can regain the courage to "think outside the box." I am praying that I will no longer be captive to the rigid standards of the world or the rigid traditions of the religious culture. I pray for the courage to allow the Holy Spirit to minister life to me afresh.

I am certain of this one thing: God wants all of God's daughters to dance and dance and dance some more. I feel the Lord calling us from the staleness, fatigue, and restriction that fall into our lives. God is granting us divine permission to enter into a spiritual place of moving and flowing with God and a place of knowing that we can live bigger than we are living. Even as we are dealing with pain, conflict, and loss, we have the blessed assurance that God is working in all things for our good. Just as God parted the Red Sea to deliver Moses and the Israelites from their enemies, God is clearly committed to our mind and spirit to overcome the forces within and without that inhibit our ability to dance.

Sisters who dance know that we do not have to be a carbon copy of anyone; we have our own style. We are unique combinations of individuality and spiritual maturity. We are not uptight when things do not go according to our plans. Women who dance do not fit into molds, and they have the audacity to be brilliant, confident, talented, and "in charge." We will not shrink so that others will not feel insecure around us. We will consistently manifest the glory of God. We will let our lights shine. We will stretch our own minds and give our sisters space and permission to do the same.

Let us look at the text in 2 Samuel. It was a day David had long dreamed of. He was king of Israel and Judah after successfully defeating the Philistines. Israel was now a strong nation, free of Philistine rule. The ark of the covenant, which had been captured by the Philistines and had been in the home of Abinidab for many years was back in the possession of the Israelites. The ark was being returned to Jerusalem to be placed in a tent prepared by David. Its return was a day of celebration and jubilation, because it represented to the Israelites God's presence, the availability of God's power, and rest from their enemies. As God had promised, the city of David would be "[God's] resting place." On this very special day, the Bible says that David laid aside his royal robes and, adorned in a mere tunic, "danced before the LORD with all of his might."

The word *dance* as used in the ancient text means to leap for joy, to rejoice, to delight in the Lord. This dance was neither a ritualistic dance nor merely a natural response to a soul-stirring beat. This was not an ordinary Sabbath worship celebration; it was a dance of reconnection. It was a dance of rediscovery. This dance was a dance that said, "I have been through a lot. I have been down to the depths of despair. I have hurt some folks and been hurt by some folks. I have experienced the divine protection of God, and I have received the forgiveness of God. And now I feel the breath of God sustaining me and pushing me into the safety of God's arms."

How long had it been since David had danced—really danced? In the preceding years, his life had taken many turns. He had fought his enemies, dealt with a paranoid father-in-law, hid out in caves and in the wilderness, and lost his best friend, Jonathan, in a battle with the Philistines. I would imagine that David had not felt like dancing for quite some time. But now that the ark was back, a load had been taken off of his mind and spirit. He believed that the presence of the ark was a guarantee of blessing and victory and deliverance from their enemies. It symbolized to him a fulfillment of God's promise to provide divine protection in the midst of it all. And so he danced.

The Bible says that David's wife Michal was offended by his display. Something in her made her "unmovable," such that she could not appreciate or identify with David's joy or lack of restraint. She accused him of being out of control and acting more like a servant than a king.

How had Michal gotten to this place? There was a time when Michal had been on top of the world. Like most of us who are high on life, she undoubtedly had been a dancer. First Samuel 18:20 reveals that Michal had been young, in love, and optimistic. Her father, Saul, was the king of the land. She had servants at her beck and call, and a young warrior named David was willing to risk his life just to take her as his wife. I have to believe that Michal was a dancer who was living the "high life." But then "stuff happened." Her father wanted to kill her husband, and her husband was constantly running from her father. She was a woman "caught in the middle." She soon understood that her father was using her. David was so absorbed in running from Saul that he was physically and emotionally unavailable to her. As a result, she resented David and had lost her dance.

She used to dance, but now she sat in a window bitter and encumbered. She used to have lightness of spirit, but a season of trying to please others and being used and pushed aside had understandably moved her to a place of rage and spiritual drought. When I look at Michal, I see a woman all of us can become and a woman all of us should fight not to become. Trouble has come and tears have fallen, but we cannot allow anything to restrict our soul. And so I have made up in my mind that in spite of whatever is going on in my life, I am ready to dance again.

Like David I want to be able to be free, loose, and wild. When the ark of the covenant was returned, it did not matter to David that he was a king, a warrior, or a priest; he had to dance. I seek to occupy such a place. Despite my responsibilities as a wife, mother, pastor, and preacher, I still want to be a dancer. I want to be unreserved and free-flowing again. I want to trade in my sorrow, my pain, and my frustration to once again feel God's presence.

Some of us need to think of ourselves beyond our roles and responsibilities in life. In the presence of the Lord, you are not a lawyer, a doctor, a teacher, or a first lady; *you are a dancer*. You are not a singer, a banker, or a wife; *you are a dancer*. Choose not to be conventional. Choose not to hide out in safe places. Choose to make up your own steps. Don't be like Michal and allow the "David" in your life to restrict you. For as sure as he is a man, David is going to do his thing, whether you like it or not. And so no "David," no job, no painful experience should consume you or make you one of life's wallflowers. You can dance again.

I am calling for dancers—ones who are sure that the presence of the Lord is here to transform their lives, those who have fought off feelings of intimidation and will not be conformed by public opinion. The Lord is releasing an anointing that will empower every Michal in the community of the faithful to discover the treasure within, escape her bondage, learn to love herself again, and find the courage to be intolerant of anything or any person who is robbing her of an authentic and intimate relationship with God.

God is calling us to a faith and inner peace that are manifested in dance. God is restoring us to our former selves, giving us a faith and assurance that eliminate feelings of intimidation in our lives. When we dance again, just as Moses told Caleb, the land on which our feet dance will be our inheritance and that of our children. Our dance will sanctify the place where our feet touch and will call that which is wrong into divine order. We must dance again. We must dance ourselves out of religious and denominational tradition, human expectations, and family skeletons.

It's your time to be light again. It's your time to dance. The wait is over and the sun is about to shine again. Keep on praising the Lord until the shackles fall off. Enter into God's presence and experience increase. Feel the love and acceptance of God and know that you are being recreated anew. Get ready to dance again!

12

When Women Have Wings
Zechariah 5:5-11

*And [the angel] said. "This is Wickedness." So he thrust her
back into the basket, and pressed the leaden weight down
on its mouth. Then I looked up and saw two women
coming forward. The wind was in their wings; they had
wings like the wings of a stork, and they lifted up the
basket between earth and sky.*
—Zechariah 5:8-9

The book of Zechariah is a prophetic writing intended to encourage the people of Judah to resume the building of the temple and complete it in the name of the God of the Israel. The Jews had come out of Babylonian captivity, their bondage had ended, and now it was time for the people of God to return to God. From the Israelite perspective, the people were living under a curse that had been brought on by their disobedience, and this curse would be lifted if the people moved into right relationship with God and established themselves as a worshiping community. The fundamental message of the prophet Zechariah was that the salvation and liberation of the people could be accomplished with worship, sacrifice, and obedience.

Zechariah is a book wrought with visions. The imagery and the metaphors found in the visions generally express God's displeasure with sin in the life of the believer. The overriding message of the book rings loudly in the ear of the men and women of God: that according to the plan of God, all who call on his name must never allow sin to control or dominate their lives.

The "woman in the basket" text in Zechariah 5:5-11 has always been problematic for me. My feminist/womanist underpinnings compel me to resent the notion of a woman being housed in a basket. This image of a woman being squeezed into a basket is uncomfortable for me because this picture is one that seems to convey confinement, oppression, restriction and invisibility. The vision of a woman in the basket is one that conjures a woman forced to be immobile, silent, and constrained in a place that is unnatural and detrimental. To be in a basket is to know affliction and pain and misery. No woman ought to find herself in a basket.

And then, to hear that the woman represents "wickedness" is even more distressing and discomforting, for of course, I must ask the question, "Why must it be a female who is characterized as evil?" Is this text a product of sexism? Does this picture reinforce the belief that women must be controlled, suppressed, and "put into a basket" because of their failure to comply or align themselves with patriarchal notions of "goodness"?

But even as I struggle with the notion of vision of evil as a woman in a basket, I am also compelled to deal with two realities. First, honesty would dictate that even the most dedicated womanist thinker must admit that there are some women in this world who have given themselves over to "evil." Their actions, their thoughts, and their conversations are grounded in malice and wickedness. There are women whose deeds have yielded horrendous pain, suffering, and despair. Women have victimized, mistreated, and destroyed. Names such as Bonnie Parker (of Bonnie and Clyde infamy), Ma Barker, and Karla Faye Tucker have all gone down in history as women who were heartless and cruel. Like it or not, evil finds its place in the heart of women.

As much as I do not like to admit it, there are some women who clearly have evil intentions. For years we have seen "evil" women wreak havoc in the church of the living God. Viciously fighting and ridiculing the pastor, subtly or overtly fighting the program of the church, they are more committed to demoralizing the leadership than living for God. They have no reverence for the church, no fear of God, and no respect for the notion of righteousness or holiness. Their intention is simply to have things their way.

Yes, some women are by their very nature determined to be the undoing of others. They are controlled by spirits of anger, rage, and jealousy and they intentionally injure and shatter lives. They beat children, attack their neighbors, and hurt other women. They make the lives of their coworkers or employees miserable and look for ways to hurt and wound. One reality I must acknowledge in my reading of this text is that there are some women who are so reprobate and depraved that they are in baskets of emotional detachment, and are in dire need of being transformed, healed, and delivered.

The second truth this text forces us to see is that this woman in the basket represents the part of all who are oppressed and attacked by sin. We don't belong there, but because of our bad choices, because of unfortunate circumstances, because of destructive forces, we are there nonetheless. This woman is every woman who has lived with the oppression of racism, sexism, classism, and political self-interest. She is the woman who is controlled by her hatred, her unforgiveness, her addiction, or her temper. She is every woman restricted by her undisciplined behavior, or insatiable appetite for power and human recognition. This woman in the basket is the woman who allows her children to take advantage of her, her mate to disrespect her, or repeatedly permits family members to use her. She is the young woman who cannot forget her experiences of rape, incest, or emotional abuse, so she lives beneath her potential because she feels there is something wrong with her. She is that woman who wants to hold her head up and move beyond her past, but guilt and shame keep her in bondage. The truth is many of us have lived in the basket.

Many of us are in baskets of our own creation. We find ourselves in places of confinement and restriction because of the disorder in our lives. Some are in the basket because of the lies they have told and tried to live. Some are there because they have overspent and neglected to tithe, and are now drowning in debt. Many sisters are living in a basket because they have given into spirits of depression, bitterness, and unforgiveness. Others have given in to the inclination to esteem destructive personalities and listen to the wrong voices. Still others have refused to grow up and act responsibly. They are in occupational ruts, but will not go back to school; they have given birth to daughters, but personal issues have distracted them and their children have gone "unmothered."

To be sure, as much as I would want to assert that this image of a woman in the basket was unfair and an invention of Zechariah's misogynist attitude, honesty forces me to admit that the symbolism herein, is representative of the female experience. Evil forces in life—forces from without *and* within—have throughout time have restricted and constrained women. The truth is, women and men alike, have all known "basket existence."

And when this Scripture describes the woman trying to get out of the basket and the angel pushing her back in, the imagery is a harsh reminder that the evil in our lives must be contained. We cannot allow it to run rampant; it cannot be a controlling force. It must be stifled. It must be suppressed. It must be quelled. The evil in our lives should be relegated to the basket so the rest of who we are can be free.

But our reading of this text must not stop with the woman in the basket, for there are two states of being represented here. To be sure, there is the woman in the basket, but in this pericope there are also some *women with wings*. Zechariah declares: "Then I looked up and saw two women coming forward. The wind was in their wings; they had wings like the wings of a stork, and they lifted up the basket between the earth and the sky. Then I said, 'Where are they taking the basket?' Then the angel said, 'To the land of Shinar.'"

There were some women with wings who lifted up the woman in the basket, who took control of evil and carried it off to another place. It is the women with wings who are the women we must be—the women who we must become.

This text seems to remind us that there are two kinds of women in this world: there are women in baskets—women who are oppressed, restricted, and confined, and there are women with wings—women who will not be confined or crushed by their circumstances, women who commit to lifting themselves out of states of being that are designed to keep them repressed and overpowered by inside and outside forces. This pericope reminds us that we have power over wickedness. We have the wherewithal to lift and carry our sister who is confined and oppressed by the situations of life.

And now I can see that this Scripture is not as anti-female as I have thought. Another reading of this text shows us that as women, we have choices. We can choose to live in states of oppression and bondage, or we can have wings!

When your hope is in God and not in the flesh, you have wings. When you do not worry about the opinion of others because you know "my help comes from the LORD" (Psalm 121:2), you have wings. When you give the Lord control of your life and decide to identify and eliminate mental bondages from your life, you will have wings. When you are transformed by the renewing of your mind, you will have wings. And when you have wings, you will not be overcome by trouble, but you will overcome trouble with the peace of God that passes all understanding.

Zechariah helps us to see it is the women with wings that we must become. While we may have known basket existences, we can be set free. We will live authentically when we refuse to be controlled by sin, and are able to resist the temptations of self-destructive spirits in our midst. Women with wings are not weak or afraid. They are committed to their own liberation and to the liberation of other women. They do not pollute the temple but cleanse it; they do not destroy but build up. They are free because they work to ensure that they are not defined by their problems, mistakes or heartbreaks. They are relentless in their fight to be healed and restored through the power of God. And their faith tells them that because of Jesus, because of the death and resurrection of the Savior, they are not defeated by ungodly systems, but can fly high. Their ever present motivation is one truth: "Greater is he that is in me than he that is in the world" (1 John 4:4).

And like the women in the text, we who are of the faith have "wind beneath our wings"—the wind of the Holy Spirit. We have the spirit of God that moves us from sin to salvation, from slavery to freedom. The Lord gives us the help we need to fly.

I thank God for my wings. They have kept me in the midst of persecution, discrimination, heartbreak, and disappointment. Wings have given me and many women the resilience, strength, and feistiness to transcend our limitations. Our wings have helped us live by faith and not by sight, and move ahead with the assurance that the "Lord will make a way somehow."

Broken and bruised, but still we rise. Often knocked to our knees, but still we rise. Persecuted, lied on, and crushed by problems, but still we rise. In her famous poem, Maya Angelou says it for us. Some shoot with a word, cut with a look, kill with hate, but still like air, we rise.

When women have wings, we know that we have the potential to get up and improve that which is detrimental. We can run and not be weary, walk and not faint (Isaiah 40:31). We can escape from the enemies who would imprison us in the things of the flesh. We will not be swallowed by our problems, and we demand respect and will take on challenges with creativity. We are resourceful, determined, and wise. We are peacemakers and repairers of the breach. When women have wings, we have healing in our hands—a healing that comes because we have a new heart and a new spirit. When trouble comes, we fly straight to the arms of Jesus. And the good news is that though we may never be one of the power brokers of the land, we do have the power to mount up on wings as eagles and soar to places unimagined. Because Jesus Christ is the hope of glory, we are continually being renewed into better ways of being; we are continually released from our basket existence to achieve new heights where we may experience and enjoy God.

13

I Can't Live Here Anymore

Genesis 38:6-30

Tamar was told, "Your father-in-law is going up to Timnah to shear his sheep," she put off her widow's garments, put on a veil, wrapped herself up, and sat down at the entrance to Enaim, which is on the road to Timnah. She saw that Shelah was grown up, yet she had not been given to him in marriage.
—Genesis 38:13-14

My life changed forever when I came to realize that I did not have to follow the world's script for my life. My world took on new meaning when I came to understand that I did not have to follow the path that everyone else followed. I grew up a well behaved little girl. I lived within the realm of other folks' expectations and dreams. I did not know how to dream "out of the box" because I did not comprehend the possibility that life could exceed human definition. My life changed when I understood that I did not have to be anybody but who God created me to be.

Something began to happen to me when I began to read about Vashti and Esther, Miriam and Deborah, Harriet Tubman and Sojourner Truth, and other women who made major contributions to their worlds. When I heard Aretha Franklin sing "R-E-S-P-E-C-T," I understood the woman I had to become. And when I embraced the reality that strong, unconventional women can save a nation and turn the world upside down, things began to happen in me.

I was about to drown out my potential with safe thinking and conventional notion of womanhood, but then one day God showed me something more. God showed me how to go after the gift of God in me, and God gave me permission *not* to be the "well behaved" woman with whom most people are comfortable.

History attests to the reality that well behaved folks seldom change systems or begin new movements. Women who back down in the face of opposition or trouble rarely break glass ceilings or move beyond the status quo. Sometimes a woman has to do what a woman has to do. People will call you pushy and out of control, but when you decide that you cannot live in places of conventionality and compromise, your world will begin to expand. You just cannot be well behaved all the time.

I am praying that in this season there are some sisters who, like Rosa Parks, are tired of sitting at the back of the bus. The call is for some folk who are being suffocated by a certain relationship or circumstance. There is a need for the teen who has lost control of her life and the sister who is bored or frustrated with her life to go after a better way of living. We all must remember that we have God's permission to go after health and wellness and significance, and today is the day to move.

Don't worry when people have a lot to say about it or try to keep you in places of restrictive living, because I can assure you that the door is open, the way has been cleared, and *you don't have to live in the places of inferiority or self-destruction.* You can leave that gang. You can leave that abusive relationship. You can vacate that dead end situation. Make up in your mind: "*I can't live here anymore.* I cannot allow unfortunate circumstances to enslave me and thus, destroy the new dimensions of self that are in me. I cannot back down from the person that I am."

There are some women whose souls have been crushed to the point that they have retreated into themselves, retreated from God, and not demanded anything of themselves that would bring on a new beginning. All of us need to remember that there is more to life than we are currently experiencing. There is a new and better self in all of us, but stuff won't begin to happen the way it *can* happen until we make some daring choices.

Decide that you are going to deal with your past (as dark or conflicted as it may be) in such a way that it brings out the hidden gift and buried treasure in you. There is more to you than meets the eye, but sometimes you don't know it is there until trouble opens the door to other parts of our soul. It is not God's desire for you to get stuck.

Now let me warn you that Satan does not want you to discover the treasures that lie within you, so he will alienate you from yourself so you remain undeveloped. When we fall into depression, doubt, low self-esteem, no self-discipline, *we die and do not grow.* Thus, Satan, the arch deceiver, has polluted our thoughts and hearts with so much anger, unforgiveness, and fear that many of us have not been able to let the character, hope and possibilities in our souls to come alive. We are functioning far beneath our spiritual, professional, and emotional potential because we have not realized the full measure of what is inside us—the treasure that will usher us into the life God intended.

If the story of Tamar teaches us anything, it shows us that we cannot allow the abuses or insensitivity of other people, even the ones we love, to keep us from letting God fill us with the Spirit's presence. Tamar reminds us that our elevation and advancement will not come unless we *fight back.* Her life reveals that trouble will cause a revolution of the soul—a revolution that will either separate us from God or align us with God. Tamar shows us that it is up to us how we allow life's struggles and hits to impact us, and she reminds us that we must maintain a faith-filled perspective if we want to be transformed to a new time and place in God.

The story of Tamar intrigues me because I see her as a woman whose experience is not validated by biblical history. Most scholars describe Tamar simply as a deceptive and godless woman who tricked her father-in-law and used him to give her the offspring she so desperately wanted. But as I have looked at her through the years, I find that Tamar is a woman who went through a lot but who ultimately decided that she would step out of traditional place of oppression and convention and make some waves. She was a woman who woke up one day and realized that if she was going to get anywhere, she would have to take charge of her life, secure her future, and pursue her place in history. She chose an unconventional escape from her misery and entered into her place of purpose.

When we look at Tamar's tale, we see that for most of the story, she is a woman caught in a web of tragedy, deception, and family duplicity. She married into a family that did not have great regard for her; she was widowed twice, and then she was pushed aside and expected to accept a barren future without a fight. She was told to forget her dreams and stifle her potential—all for the sake of keeping the peace.

But Tamar had a little bit more "gumption" than they gave her credit for. She absolutely refused to be a "good girl." She battled the demons of tradition and compliance, and she defined herself, determined her future, and discovered parts of herself that had been hidden far too long. She realized that she had more nerve than she had imagined, more ingenuity than she had ever explored, and a whole lot of courage that her traditional, gender-appropriate role had stifled.

In short, Tamar was a woman who wanted more out of life than other folks were willing to give her, so she decided that she had to get up out of her place of waiting, connect with herself, and stretch out. Life gets better when a woman begins to say to herself, "It is time for me to stretch and grow! I cannot take this anymore. I am getting him out of my system. I am getting ready to move from this place!"

The Bible says Judah chose Tamar as the wife of his oldest son, Er. From all that I can discern, Er was a terrible man—mean, nasty, and probably abusive. So horrible was he that his life was cut short, and Tamar found herself a widow. And then according to the levirate marriage law, Judah sent his second son, Onan, to Tamar, with instructions to procreate and provide a son to perpetuate Er's bloodline. Now the Bible tells us that Onan was not happy about the notion of producing an heir for his dead brother, so when he was in the throes of lovemaking, just before he was to experience orgasm, he would withdraw and spill his seed on the ground. He was so selfish that God killed him too.

Once again Tamar was left without husband or child. No doubt Judah blamed Tamar for killing his sons, but the way I see it, both young men were so wretched that God mercifully delivered Tamar out of her miserable marriages! Now Judah had a third son, a young boy by the name of Shelah, who by law should have become Tamar's husband. But because of Shelah's youth, Judah sent Tamar back to her father's house, supposedly to wait until Shelah came of age, and promised to send for her at the appropriate time. Tamar should never have trusted Judah, because if you remember Judah is a son of Jacob (the deceiver) and brother of Joseph. Judah was one of the brothers who put Joseph in the pit, sold him into slavery, and claimed that their father's favorite was dead. Without a doubt, Judah had a lineage and a history of lying, self-serving cruelty, and hypocrisy.

Seeing no options, however, a humiliated and crushed Tamar went back to her father's house and waited. Shelah soon came of age, but Judah did not send for Tamar. And she waited and waited. Twice widowed, childless, and because of her tie to Judah's family, ineligible to marry any other man, and there she was, existing on the fringes of life, with no place to become; suspended between a miserable reality and a desire to reach divine significance.

If you have ever lived on the fringes, you understand why Tamar knew she had to get up out of there. There was something brewing deep inside Tamar, and she knew that she was not going to just sit back and surrender her dreams. She was not going to allow herself to be a victim of one man's lack of integrity.

We have all had to struggle to overcome the setbacks that life has dealt us. When we could have given up, something on the inside kept fighting to break out. When things were falling apart, a determination deep in our souls let us know that we had not been conquered. The spirit of Tamar compels us to tire of working to become who others want us to become and fight to become the woman *God* made us to be? Her legacy to us is an understanding that in order to live, we might have to step out of character, and get outrageous, unconventional and even a little bit crazy. Every woman that God created has a calling, an anointing, and a plan that must be manifested in our lives.

The Bible says that Tamar devised a plan. By this time Judah was a widower himself. His wife had died, and after a period of mourning, he went to visit a buddy of his who lived not far from Tamar's father. When she heard that her father-in-law was on his way to nearby Timnah, Tamar took off her widow's garments, put on a veil, wrapped herself up, and sat down by the side of the road to wait. Along came Judah and when he saw Tamar, he didn't recognize her.

As a matter of fact, he assumed she was a prostitute and propositioned her.

Tamar responded in turn: "What will you give me if I come to you?" When Judah promised to send a kid from his flock once he returned home, she said that a promise wasn't good enough and demanded some collateral. And so Scripture says Judah gave her his signet, his cord, and his staff, and then he "went in to her." That night Tamar conceived. Judah later sent the goat he had promised, wanting to recover his belongs, but the mysterious "prostitute" was nowhere to be found.

About three months later, Judah got the word that his daughter-in-law, Tamar, was pregnant. "Bring her here and let her be burned," he declared. When his servants came for her, Tamar responded by sending the signet, the cord, and the staff ahead with the message, "It was the owner of these things who made me pregnant."

Of course, then Judah realized what had happened, and he had to repent his lack of character and the deception he had perpetrated against Tamar. Judah was stripped of his arrogance and selfishness and assumed full responsibility for his family. And Tamar soon gave birth to twin boys named Perez and Zerah.

So now Tamar was vindicated; God had worked it out that she be exonerated from her death sentence and given an opportunity to leave a place of barrenness in pursuit of a righteous cause. For you see, had Tamar not given birth to Perez, there would have been no Boaz. Had there been no Boaz, there would have been no Obed; had there been no Obed, there would have been no Jesse, and had there been no Jesse, there would have been no David.

And so we celebrate this woman who could have been lost in the pages of history, never to emerge again. But because she thought more highly of herself than her culture did, she did not internalize defeat. Instead, she got bold and resourceful and decided to move from victim to victor. And in her struggle to survive, she connected to God's better way.

This story challenges us to safeguard our relationship with God and with ourselves. No matter how much we mess up or are messed over, we can allow God to fill our empty places with his divine healing. We cannot allow anyone's abuse, lies or rejection keep her from finding the richness of character and potential that is in her. We must be the modern day Tamars who are willing to stand up and refuse to be controlled by fear, stereotypical images, or societal bondages and oppression. We have the potential birth to new possibilities and become spiritually creative and productive. We must assume our place in kingdom order.

Through the years women have been marginalized, treated unfairly, and emotionally violated, but many have been steadfast in their resolve not to allow opponents to stand in the way of becoming what God has called us to be. Life will bring hurt feelings, lost loves, and difficult relationships, but we dare not miss out on what God will do in us by giving up too soon. Broken marriages, unfaithful spouses, absent fathers, or abusive mothers may be the source of pain or setbacks, but God's love and vision for God's women is unwavering. We possess a creative genius that makes it possible for us to move from other-inflicted prisons to the courts of the Lord. We are each one of God's chosen daughters, made in God's image, and too anointed and valuable to live on the fringes. Therefore, we cannot allow the Judahs of the world to control us or keep us away from the destiny that is ours. Let us commit to pursue our God-ordained place in this world!

A Concluding Word

The Bible continues to be an instrument of liberation for the African American Christian community. Though scholars, preachers, and laypeople alike have established that certain texts are inexcusably oppressive to women, it is the task of the womanist reader to extract from the whole of the biblical text a meaning and interpretation that provides liberation and hope for all of humanity. It is imperative that African American female readers understand that biblical interpretation is subjective and can emerge as the result of their own experience and tradition. It is the responsibility of womanist theologians to develop personal reading strategies and interpretations that reject traditional interpretations that have sought to diminish or devalue African American women. We must find in the Bible a divine hope and promise that consistently affirm African American women's humanity and give them a positive presence in the text. The Bible is authoritative and liberating in the lives of African American women only when our interpretive process allows our voices to be proclaimed and our faces to be uncovered within that text that we have come to love and value.

Epilogue

The gospel of Jesus Christ provides hope for renewal and personal empowerment that must be revealed in sermon. My commitment to women's ministry remains grounded in my respect for and sensitivity to every aspect of the African American female experience as well as my belief that those who preach must intentionally deconstruct and denounce biblical interpretations that oppress women and create false perceptions for men.

I have spent years seeking to develop sermons that address the needs and realities of women. I believe that it is my responsibility to facilitate the transformation, healing, and liberation of women through preaching and programming. Whether in Sunday morning worship or at a midweek women's service, sermons that affirm the personhood of women, in spite of painful realities and past experiences, and proclaim a gospel that empowers and transforms broken and spiritually oppressed woman are a powerful means through which broken spirits are restored, self-esteem is renewed, and expectations are expanded.

The power and success of sermon lie in the conveyance of an understanding that lives can be and ought to be transformed. It is important for preachers, pastors, and theologians to identify the negative and oppressive aspects of our culture, political realities, and church traditions and practices. Black women's experiences with gender inequality, racism, rape, and other forms of violence must be addressed on systemic levels and must, therefore, be on the church's overall agenda. However, for sermon to stop there would be a disservice to the people of God. I am convinced more than ever that those who preach must seek continually to employ insightful and creative methodologies that inspire women and men to identify toxic relationships, self-defeating attitudes, and self-destructive behaviors. Counseling sessions and informal exchanges with hurting women confirm the need for sermons that help women to move toward wholeness. When a child has been shot to death or a husband has announced that he wants to end a twenty-nine-year marriage, a woman needs a gospel that is healing and restorative.

Unfortunately, the twenty-first-century church's new emphasis on a theology of prosperity and economic growth has the potential to create an atmosphere that is insensitive to the realities of women who are experiencing dysfunctional relationships, dealing with memories of rape or incest, or receiving chemotherapy every week. Many women will confirm that a new car or the promise of a new house is not the source of the strength they need to deal with their hurts nor a message that gives them the will to move through the dark seasons of their lives. They need sermonic experiences that contain a call to personal transformation and remind them that salvation and healing are available regardless of past or present circumstances. Clearly, every sermon is not required to address "women's issues," but every sermon is required to set the stage for divine encounter and a message that conveys the promise of hope, joy, and wholeness. Thus, my commitment will always be to engage in biblical interpretation and sermon development that supports the growth and healing of every area of the lives of God's women.

It is my hope that this work has restored or created a new resolve among God's servants, ministerial and lay, to strive to assure that every woman everywhere finds God in her midst.

Additional Preaching Resources from Judson Press

Speak until Justice Wakes: Prophetic Reflections from
J. Alfred Smith Sr. by J. Alfred Smith Sr.
From one of the most respected statesmen in the African American
church comes an inspirational resource that communicates with
unbridled passion what it means to speak truth to power.
978-0-8170-1501-5 $11.00

The Star Book on Preaching by Marvin A. McMickle
In the classic tradition of the best-selling *The Star Book for Ministers*,
McMickle offers the keys to an effective preaching ministry.
978-0-8170-1492-6   Hardcover $14.00

A National Best Seller!
Best Black Sermons Edited by William M. Philpot
Features twelve sermons including a classic from Martin Luther King Jr.
978-0-8170-0533-7 $12.00

**Afrocentric Sermons: The Beauty of Blackness in the Bible by
Kenneth L. Waters Sr.**
Preaching that strives to "heal the spirit of my people so that they can
rise up and be the people of God."   978-0-8170-1199-4 $12.00

**Fire in the Well Sermons by Ella and Henry Mitchell Edited by
Jacqueline B. Glass**
For the first time in one resource, experience Henry and Ella as they
address issues of concern.   978-0-8170-1447-6 $15.00

Outstanding Black Sermons, Volumes 1–4
Showcasing the best preaching in today's black churches, these sermons demonstrate the social relevance of the gospel in the black experience.
Vol. 1 edited by J. Alfred Smith Sr.   978-0-8170-0664-8 $12.00
Vol. 2 edited by Walter B. Hoard   978-0-8170-0832-1 $12.00
Vol. 3 edited by Milton E. Owens Jr.   978-0-8170-0973-1 $12.00
Vol. 4 edited by Walter S. Thomas   978-0-8170-1378-3 $14.00

Those Preaching Women, Volumes 1–4
"They are biblical communicators who bring a fresh perspective with the prophetic flair." —Bishop Vashti Murphy McKenzie
Vol. 1–3 edited by Ella Pearson Mitchell
Vol. 1   978-0-8170-1073-7 $12.00
Vol. 2   978-0-8170-1131-4 $12.00
Vol. 3   978-0-8170-1249-6 $12.00
Vol. 4 edited by Ella Pearson Mitchell and Jacqueline B. Glass
978-0-8170-1464-3 $14.00

To order, call 800-458-3766, or order online
at www.judsonpress.com.

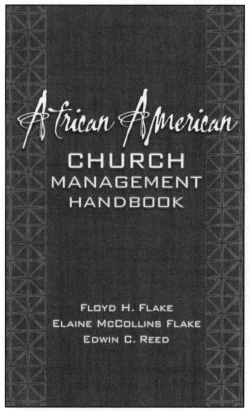